The Smalbanac

The Smalbanac

An Opinionated Guide to New York's Capital District

Christine Garretson-Persans

excelsior editions

State University of New York Press
Albany, New York

Published by
State University of New York Press, Albany

For information, contact State University of New York Press, Albany, NY
www.sunypress.edu

Production by Kelli W. LeRoux
Marketing by Fran Keneston

Library of Congress Cataloging-in-Publication Data

Garretson-Persans, Christine.
    The Smalbanac : an opinionated guide to New York's capital district / Christine
Garretson-Persans.
        p. cm.
    Includes index.
    ISBN 978-1-4384-3150-5 (pbk. : alk. paper)
    1. Albany (N.Y.)—Description and travel.   2. Albany (N.Y.)—History.   I. Title.

F129.A34G37 2010
917.47'430444—dc22   2009026797

10 9 8 7 6 5 4 3 2 1

Welcome to the **Smalbanac**! Whether you are new to the area or have been here forever, the goal of the Smalbanac is to point you to things in the capital district that make our small city something special.

We have a 400-year history marked by ingenuity, hard work, and a certain measure of curious behavior. Inside you'll find history! Drama! Science! Guides to all things practical! And of course MORE!!!!

** A Note About Our Listings **

All of the phone numbers in the Smalbanac are in the 518 area code unless otherwise noted. We have only listed places we have visited, so if you are not in this edition, don't feel bad—there's always next time. We hope to publish an updated edition every few years, so if you have comments or suggestions, please visit us at www.smalbanac.com.

Contents

Albany—400 Years Old and Counting

In 2009, Albany celebrated the 400th anniversary of Henry Hudson's arrival in the capital region. Hudson sailed the Half Moon up what would become known as the Hudson River and anchored here on September 19, 1609. Some have confused this date with the actual anniversary of Albany's beginning. Although this is indeed something to celebrate, it took a bit longer to actually get Albany off the ground. Hudson was here for only 4 days trying to figure out what to do next as his plans for sailing to Asia along the river sort of fell apart. Settlers from Holland didn't start arriving for a few years, and Fort Orange, the real start of the city, wasn't built until 1624. The city itself wasn't actually chartered until 1686. We've had centennial celebrations on the '86s for the last 300 years and a couple of centennial celebrations on the '24s. You will find parks and plaques around town to commemorate the 1686 anniversary; the real one. With that said, Hudson's arrival was most important to Albany's eventual growth, and any excuse for a celebration is a good one, so party on.

Anyway. Albany got a kick start once the Half Moon returned to the Netherlands (via England) after Hudson failed to find a northwest passage to India for the Dutch East India Co. He brought back beaver pelts and tales of the fertile land; that was enough for the Dutch to start sending over traders. The beaver had been hunted to near extinction in Europe and this area was a new source for that very popular fur. To get enough Dutch in the area to keep it from being settled by other Europeans, they adopted a patroon system where tracts of land were given to "patroons" for every 50 settlers they could bring to the area. Killian Van Rensselaer (who never set foot here) was given about 800,000 acres on either side of the river here for settling 50 adults. When the British took over in 1664 the generous terms of the settlement maintained the patroonship, except for the part that was the city of Albany, which was released from the patroon in 1668. Eventually, the beaver was hunted to near extinction here as well, at which point the land changed from hunting grounds to farmland.

Albany has been the state capital since 1777 (it was formerly in Kingston). The original name given to the area by the Dutch was Beverwijck "district of the beaver." This has been Americanized to Beverwyck. When the British took over in 1664, the name was changed to honor James II, Duke of Albany (Alba means Scotland—James was King Charles II's son and was named the duke of both York and Albany). Somewhere along the line, the city motto became "assiduity," which means perseverance with a purpose.

The Hudson River gave Albany the opportunity for all kinds of economic growth, which has molded the city over the past 400 years. Albany used to be home to the largest brewery in America. It was the largest producer of aspirin, potato chips, caps and gowns, spring beds, and toilet paper. The first depression took care of most of those businesses. Today Albany's main business is that of government.

The city itself has about 95,000 people, but approximately 1 million people live in the capital region—Albany, Troy, and Schenectady.

Here is a list of interesting places worth visiting if you're just passing through or actually live here.

Anneke Janse Bogardus plaque: No building, or statue, just a plaque on State Street, near James where her house once stood. The plaque reads, "Upon this corner stood the house occupied by and wherein died Anneke Janse Bogardus 1663." You've probably walked by this hundreds of times and maybe you've wondered who Anneke was. She was born around 1605 in Amsterdam, married Roelof Jansen, and moved to Rensselaerwyck in 1630, making her one of the earliest settlers. Within 5 or 6 years, they moved to New Amsterdam (New York City) and Roelof was given 62 acres of so-so farmland smack in the middle of what would become Manhattan. They had six children. Roelof died in 1637, within a year of his sixth child's birth. Shortly thereafter (in 1638), Anneke married the Rev. Everardus Bogardus with whom she had another four children. After the reverend died at sea on a trip to visit Amsterdam in 1647, the widow Bogardus moved back to Fort Orange to be near her daughter. She died here around February 23, 1663 and was buried next to the Old Dutch Reform Church at State and Broadway. Anneke's remains were moved to Albany Rural by 1867. She left her 62 acres in Manhattan to her children, but somehow the land ended up in the hands of Trinity Church and it has been in litigation since the 1700s with only the lawyers making any money. There are dozens of Anneke Janse and Everardus Bogardus descendent associations across America. She apparently has approximately 1 million heirs.

Fort Crailo: 9 1/2 Riverside in Rensselaer, 463-8738. Fort Crailo was built in 1712 by Hendrick Van Rensselaer on the 1,500-acre estate that was part of his grandfather Killian's original patroonship. It had a small fort on the property dating back to the 1600s and was used for the quartering of troops during various wars. It was during the French and Indian War that a British surgeon, housed here alongside the colonists, wrote the song "Yankee Doodle" to make fun of the rather rag-tag appearance of the locals. Hendrick's granddaughter Catherine Van Rensselaer, who would eventually marry Philip Schuyler, was raised here. Fort Crailo was working on a new display in 2009. Call for hours.

The Hudson River/Hudson River Way: The Hudson River begins at Lake Tear of the Clouds on the southwest slope of Mount Marcy in the Adirondacks and flows for 315 miles. The 160 miles of navigable water north of Manhattan brought Henry Hudson to what became Albany. Recorded history of the area begins here in about 1300 AD and is based on legends of the Lenni Lenape Indians who were searching for a river that flowed both ways; which the Hudson does because it is an estuary, a tidal river that has both fresh and salt water. Steamboats once traveled up and down the river to bring people back and forth from New York City as well as to get them to Troy. From the waterfront you could look up the hill to the capitol. That is, until the Empire State Plaza came to town with its massive highway maze blotting out the entire view. Thankfully, the Hudson River Way was built in 2002 and now you can actually get to the riverfront to enjoy its beauty. The River Way brings you over the highway to miles of hiking trails, an amphitheater for warm weather music, and a breathtaking view of one of the most beautiful rivers in the world.

HALF MOON II

Love Many. Trust a Few.
Always Paddle Your Own Canoe.

Union Station: Now the Peter D. Kiernan Plaza, on Broadway between Columbia and Steuben streets, Union Station opened on December 17, 1900. It was designed by the Shepley, Rutan, and Coolidge firm and built by the Norcross Brothers. It took about 2 years to complete. The carved eagle and figures surrounding the clock took 3 months alone. Hundreds of trains passed through Albany each week. New York Central Railroad had plans to abandon it when part of its rail yards were needed for the construction of the I 787 highway. The last train left the station on December 29, 1968 almost exactly 68 years after its opening. Gov. Nelson Rockefeller bought the building with state funds in 1966; however, from 1968 to 1984 it was left to rot on the city's landscape, in part because there were no funds to do anything with it. Mayor Erastus Corning wanted the building preserved for sentimental reasons as well as historic ones. His great-grandfather had founded the New York Central Railroad. Finally, Norstar Bancorp chairman Peter D. Kiernan brought the city an acceptable plan. The bank would buy, completely renovate, and make the old Union Station its headquarters; hence, the new name of the building. Renovations began in 1984, the building reopened in 1986, and now Bank of America (formerly Norstar) has abandoned it once again.

St. Josephs: 10 Broeck Street, Albany. Patrick Keely (famous for his designs of Catholic churches) designed the gothic St. Joseph's, which was completed in 1860. St. Joseph's was built to serve the growing Irish population. When the Irish neighborhood was demolished for the Empire State Plaza and the residents headed for the suburbs, St. Joseph's no longer had the congregation to sustain it. It was sold and leased back to the church, which had its last service in 1993. The church was then sold to a private individual who had plans to turn the building into a club or disco. The building was rapidly deteriorating when the city of Albany took it over. The city transferred the property to the Historic

Albany Foundation, which has been working overtime to preserve this beautiful piece of Albany's past. If you want to help save Albany's past too, you can become a member of the foundation or just volunteer. You can call Historic Albany Foundation at 465-0876.

United Traction Building: 600 Broadway, Albany. This is another one of those beautiful buildings designed by Marcus T. Reynolds (SUNY Plaza). The United Traction Company was a consolidation of the Albany Railway, the Troy City Railway, and the Watervliet Turnpike and Railroad Company. The companies signed the merger on December 30, 1899, the same year the new headquarters was built. United Traction was plagued by strikes, the most notable being the strike in May 1901 in which 3,000 militiamen were called in to subdue the strikers. This was followed by strikes in 1918 and 1921—the last one lasting a year and immortalized in the movie *Ironweed*. The last trolley run in Troy was in 1933, and in Albany it was in 1946. The bus system eventually became the Capital District Transportation Authority (CDTA). The United Traction Building became the Peter Schuyler Building (named after Albany's first mayor) and now mostly houses law offices.

The City Gardeners: Take a look around the city and you can really appreciate just how hard Judy Stacey and her unbelievable crew work to make its landscape beautiful. Every green space, every flowerpot, and every single one of those tens of thousands of tulips growing in Washington Park in May are there because this group planted them. So pay attention, look around in spring for the first display of color, and thank the City Gardeners for creating something worth looking at.

The Spectrum 8 Theaters: 290 Delaware Avenue, 449-8995. This is the best movie theater around. It took over its present location, the former

Delaware Theater in 1983. It now houses eight small theaters of assorted sizes that show an assortment of independent, semi-blockbusters and the occasion real blockbuster if it's good enough. The snack bar sells popcorn with REAL butter and great brownies and cookies. The staff is friendly and very cinema savvy. The art displayed is from local artists or galleries. And if this isn't enough, there are two parking lots for off-street parking. Tickets are $8.75; however, Tuesdays are "cheap day" with an all-day ticket price of $7. Buy a 10-pass for $70 and "cheap day" can be any day you want it to be.

The Home Savings Bank: 11 North Pearl Street. At the time of its construction in 1927, the Home Savings Bank was, at 19 stories high, the tallest building in Albany. Within 1 year, the Alfred E. Smith building surpassed it. The Home Savings Bank remains one of the most interesting old banks in Albany because of the terra cotta and gold-colored art deco designs on its top. We always wondered what Spanish Conquistadors and Sioux Indians had to do with Albany history, which is nothing by the way, but the sculptor who designed the frieze, Rene Paul Chambellan, was one of the most popular art deco designers of the time. Apparently, it didn't matter in the least to him whether the artwork was truly symbolic to this area as long as it looked really cool. Which it does.

The State Education Department: 89 Washington Avenue across from the capitol. The State Education building was the vision of Dr. Andrew Draper, New York's first commissioner of education. He wanted to build a temple to education and after a design competition, the Palmer and Hornbostle architectural firm was hired to do just that. Construction began in 1908 and was completed in 1911, although not dedicated until the following year. The 36-column colonnade across the front is the longest in the United States and one of the longest in the world. Originally, the State Museum and State Library both were housed upstairs. You could have come to visit the Cohoes mastodon with his furry friend until 1976 when it was dismantled and put into storage at the new State Museum at Empire State Plaza. (He's up again in the South Hall Lobby at the museum.) The State Education building has an amazing rotunda with a 70-foot chandelier hanging in it. There are murals, vaulted ceilings, readings rooms; all pretty outstanding. But unless you work in the building you won't get past the lobby. There is a brochure with pictures available at the information desk downstairs. Charles Keck designed the electroliers (lamp posts) that are outside the building. He used his nieces and nephews as the models for the studious kids sitting around them. You can stop by and admire the grandeur of it all, at least from the outside.

Alfred E. Smith Building: South Swan Street. The Alfred E. Smith building was built between 1927 and 1930 and was named for a four-term governor who also had the misfortune to be the democratic party's nominee for president in 1928 (Herbert Hoover was the other guy). The building has 34 stories. At 388-feet high, it was the tallest building in Albany until the Corning Tower was built. During construction of the Smith building, if you looked at the site from the river (when we had a river that you could look up from), it looked as if the long-forgotten dome was being added to the State Capitol building. Its 4-year renovation was completed in 2006. Everything was spiffed up, including the lobby's ceiling mural of famous New Yorker's by noted local mural painter David Lithgow. The outside facade with all 62 New York counties engraved in it is really a nice touch for the first really big state office building. If you want to go inside this building, it usually is open from 7 a.m. to 7.p.m. weekdays and you can try to guess who's painted on the ceiling.

The State Bank of Albany (formerly): 69 State Street. Currently the Bank of America, this bank is the oldest in the city and the oldest banking building to be continuously run as a bank in the United States. Originally the N.Y. State National Bank, it was founded in 1803, and up-and-coming architect Philip Hooker designed it. The building has been greatly modified over the past 200 years, but the entrance and the brass railing are from the original design. Inside, there are 10 wall murals measuring 12-feet-wide by almost 6.5-feet-high, depicting scenes from Albany's past. These include glimpses of the original Mohicans, Henry Hudson's arrival, the building of Fort Orange, and even includes a painting of Hooker presenting his plans for the design of the bank. The paintings were done by David Lithgow, the same artist who did the ceiling in the Alfred E. Smith building, the 14 murals in the Milne Building of the University of Albany downtown campus, and tons of smaller paintings, some of which are at the Albany Institute of History and Art. You can actually go inside this building and see the murals because it is open to the public during banking hours.

Albany Rural Cemetery: 48 Cemetery Avenue (off Broadway), Menands, 463-7017. When the old Dutch cemetery at the bottom of State Street started flooding on a frequent basis, it was decided that a new "rural" cemetery had to be built and the graves moved. This cemetery was incorporated in 1841 and formally dedicated in 1844. All of the churches in Albany had their own graveyards; however, by 1866 it was decided that all of the remains of old Albanians had to be moved out of town and into Albany Rural. This cemetery is really beautiful and a great place to take a walk while learning a bit about the city's history. There are a lot of interesting people buried here, including Samuel O' "One-Armed" Berry (1839–1873) who was part of a gang of murderers and thieves that included James Younger and Frank James. He died in jail after serving 7 years hard labor for committing multiple murders. Others include Troy's Henry Burden of the Ironworks fame; C.E. Dudley whose wife donated money to build the Dudley Observatory; Philip Hooker, architect; all three of the Erastus Cornings; a Quackenbush; Herman Melville's father; Ten Eyck's galore; Stephen Van Rensselaer III, the last patroon of Albany; a slew of Schuylers including Philip (one of the family headstones is installed upside down so it takes longer to read); Elisha P. Hurlbut, a New York Supreme Court judge and namesake of Hurlbut Street near the Spectrum; and of course Chester Alan Arthur, U.S. president who has one of the oddest looking angels caressing his grave with a palm frond. Look for the American Flag and you have found him.

Albany Institute of History and Art: 125 Washington Avenue, Albany, 463-4478. This is one of the oldest art museums in America. It houses an eclectic collection of artifacts, paintings, furniture, and just stuff (including a mummy) that provide a very thoughtful glimpse into Albany's past. The institute has wonderful educational programs and is very active with the City Neighbors Project. There is an admission fee, which is waived for Albany's First Friday 5 to 8 p.m. If you are looking for a special gift, there is an outstanding gift shop on the second floor.

Albany Visitor's Center: 25 Quackenbush Square, 434-0405. Quackenbush Square is located at the corner of Clinton and Broadway in Albany.

The Visitor's Center is housed half in the old water department building and half in the old pumping station building. It has a great little museum that offers a quick history of Albany and has a really good orientation film that provides an overview of the city. The Visitor's Center also houses the Henry Hudson Planetarium, which offers shows the third Saturday of every month at 11 a.m. and 1 p.m. for only $3. If you can find it, it is open 7 days a week and has a great staff to help you find your way into downtown.

Quackenbush House: 25 Quackenbush Square 1. Wouter Quackenbush was a brick maker who built a very nice house OUT OF BRICKS! in 1736. It used to be the oldest Dutch house in Albany but a few years ago another house dating back to 1732 was uncovered near the Greyhound station on Broadway. Quackenbush House is still the nicest, almost oldest Dutch house in the city. It is co-incidentally located in Quackenbush Square. The original foundation is believed to date back to the 1600s. It has housed not only generations of Quackenbushes, but bars, a hardware store, and is now home to Le Canard Enchaine (the Chained Duck), a very fine French restaurant. Quackenbush Square is located at the corner of Clinton and Broadway and may not appear on your GPS.

First Church: 110 N. Pearl Street, 463-4449. This Dutch Reformed church was built in 1798 and was designed by Hooker (Hooker designed a lot of the nicer old buildings in town). Inside is the oldest pulpit in America, sent over in 1656 for the original, First Church. This one has an hourglass on it to keep the sermons to an acceptable length. If your Sunday morning hangover keeps you from going inside, you can sit in the parking lot for their drive-in service all summer long. If you love Louis Comfort Tiffany, First Church has an absolutely gorgeous Tiffany Window inside by it offices. This was Teddy Roosevelt's church when he was governor and his pew is marked with a plaque.

St. Mary's Roman Catholic Church: 10 Lodge Street, 462-4254. St. Mary's is Albany's oldest Catholic church. It was incorporated on October 6, 1789, making it the second oldest Catholic church in New York. This is its third edifice, designed by Albany architect Charles Nichols and built in 1867 (the second was designed by Hooker). In 1895, under the eye of Fr. Clarence Walworth, St. Mary's became the first church to have electricity. He also was responsible for the installation of the 18-foot Archangel Gabriel that sits on top of the church. With each 100 years, major renovations and additions have been made. In 1896, in addition to electricity, the ceiling and upper wall murals were painted. In 1997–1998, the interior walls were restored and the gilding redone.

Albany Board of Education: In Academy Park across from the capitol (the first Albany Academy). This is another one of those buildings designed by Hooker around 1813. Herman Melville attended the academy during his Albany days, pre-*Moby Dick*. This is also where the great American scientist Joseph Henry performed his first experiments with electricity. It is surrounded by a conifer garden with more than 300 types of evergreens and no, we didn't count them but feel free.

New York State Capitol: Capitol Hill, 474-2418 (tour info). If you live here and haven't taken the tour then do it. It's free and happens Monday through Saturdays, unless one of those is a major holiday. This building cost $25 million in the late 1800s and took more than 30 years (1867–1899) to build. It is very impressive and has its share of cool stories with ghosts galore. The detail is amazing, right down to the 17 steps in the back and 77 in the front making the year 1777, which is New York's year of statehood. The statue in front is of Civil War Gen. Philip Sheridan and his horse, Rienzi. The city historian says Sheridan was born in Albany but some suggest his mother was in Ohio at the time, which would make his birth somewhat extraordinary.

Albany City Hall: 24 Eagle Street, between Pine and Lodge. While the Capitol was being built, the old city hall burned down. The stone carvers were in town and H.H. Richardson,[1] the architect working on the capitol, was asked to design a new city hall. It is made of Rhode Island granite and has some really outstanding design details. It also has a 49-bell carillon that is played at noon on Tuesdays and Wednesdays and on special occasions. The mayor's office is located inside the building. A statue of Philip Schuyler is located in front of the building.

Empire State Plaza: 98 acres of cement located between State and Madison. Corning was mayor, Rockefeller was governor. Rocky wanted a really cool legacy so he knocked down more than 1,000 buildings and moved out entire neighborhoods so he could do this. Although he was governor, Rockefeller was called the best *mayor* Albany ever had for turning the city around. The plaza is home to the state museum (really fun and has a great changing art gallery), Corning Tower with a free observation deck on the 42nd floor (one floor for each year Corning was mayor), four other towers, the Vietnam Memorial, and of course the Egg without which our skyline would not be nearly as distinctive.

Saint Peter's Church: 107 State Street, 434-3502. When the English took over from the Dutch in the 1600's they built their own church at

---

[1] Richardson was one of America's most famous architects. Richardsonian Romanesque is an actual style of design named for him. Google him and you will find his image roaming around in monk's garb. He was obsessed with all things medieval and really liked the hoody thing. If you know Boston, Richardson was the architect for Trinity Church there.

the top and in the middle of State Street. Eventually, things had to get out of the road and St. Peter's was built in its present location. This is the third edifice of which the foundation was laid on St. Peter's Day in 1859. There are beautiful memorial windows throughout the church and the first window to use flesh tone for human beings is in here too. L.C. Tiffany spent years during the 1880's developing the chemistry to give glass a painterlier palette and it is one of his windows, first on the right, that shows off this new technology. The mosaic floor is beautiful and the gargoyles outside are great. Underneath the entryway is the body of Gen. Lord Howe, an English officer killed in the French and Indian War. He was killed in early July but couldn't be shipped back to England for burial. Philip Schuyler brought his body back from Ticonderoga to be buried under the church, which makes Howe the only British lord to be buried in America.

SUNY Plaza: State and Broadway. The Delaware and Hudson (D&H) Railroad's headquarters, the Plaza built in 1914 and designed by Marcus T. Reynolds, another of Albany's notable architects. This building is cited as one of the most popular downtown buildings. What's not to like about a gigantic fairy castle along the river? One story goes that the rich and powerful of Albany granted D&H permission to build its new headquarters if it obscured their view of the Hudson, which at the time was incredibly busy, noisy, and dirty. Reynolds designed the building with the beautification of Albany in mind. He also designed the 9-foot weathervane of the Half Moon (Henry Hudson's ship in 1609), which weighs around 400 pounds and is the largest working weathervane in the United States (and one of the largest weathervanes in the world). It has carvings of things relating to almost everyone who played a part in Albany's history, including beavers. D&H Railroad sold the building to the State University of New York in the 1960's and is now the university's central administration building.

Nipper: 991 Broadway. Albany's 25-foot Nipper is the last remaining large statue of the RCA/Victor dog. It has been sitting in its current location since 1954 where it marked the top of the RTA Company, which distributed RCA products. The Arnoff Moving and Storage Company now owns the building and takes loving care of this famous landmark. The real Nipper was so named for his penchant for biting the ankles of passersby. Nipper died in 1895. Nipper looks down on the site where the last patroon of Albany lived. The Van Rensselaer estate and manor were there until 1893.

Historic Cherry Hill: 523 ½ South Pearl Street, 434-4791. Cherry Hill houses more than 20,000 objects from the Van Rensselaer–Rankin families. This adorable yellow home also comes complete with the story of lust and murder. Who needs more? (The book *Murder at Cherry Hill* is available at Cherry Hill and the Albany Visitor's Center.)

Schuyler Mansion: 32 Catherine Street (Catherine was the first Mrs. Philip Schuyler), 434-0834. The mansion was built between 1761 and 1765 and is home to many family artifacts. If you didn't have the obligatory first-grade trip to this site then be sure to visit it now. There have been some interesting tours of late, which offer a glimpse of the not-so-boring lives of Albany's founding fathers.

Ten Broeck Mansion: 9 Ten Broeck Place, 436-9826. Built to replace the original Ten Broeck home, which burned down in the fire of 1793, the Ten Broeck Mansion is a lovely Federal-style house with beautiful gardens. It hosts haunted Halloween tours and a great Christmas holiday house. In the summer, kids can dig up the backyard in archeology camp.

The Governor's Mansion: 138 Eagle Street. The current 39-room mansion was built around a privately owned 10-room house that was constructed in 1856. Sam Tilden was the first of New York's governors to live in the mansion beginning in 1875. The mansion is undergoing some "greening" up by using solar panels and curbing energy consumption. To schedule tours by appointment, call 473-7521.

Washington Park: Off Madison Avenue, between Willett and South Lake streets. This is a really beautiful city park that hosts a number of events throughout the year. It is an 81-acre park designed by Olmsted, the same man who designed New York's Central Park. There are walking paths throughout, tennis courts, some really great sculptures, including the one of Moses (by Rhind, the same artist who did the Philip Schuyler in front of City Hall), and the Lakehouse, which is where you will find FREE musical theater.

The Palace Theater: 19 Clinton Avenue at North Pearl, 465-3334. This theater opened in October 1931 and was considered one of the jewels in the RKO (Radio Keith Orpheum, in case you were wondering) chain. It had a successful run as a movie/vaudeville theater through the 1940s but as was common in much of the area, business declined and the theater failed. It closed by 1969 when it was sold to the city of Albany to be used as a civic auditorium. The murals, plaster work, chandelier, and the historic significance of a theater like this put it on the National Register of Historic Places in 1979. The 2,800-seat auditorium became known as a concert venue and also is home to the Albany Symphony Orchestra. Recent renovations have really made the theater shine again and movies are once again being shown here. Check the Web site, www.palacealbany. com, for the theater's excellent upcoming season.

What the @#%&*!

Now we all know that Beverwyck was one of the earlier names for what is now Albany. But one *very* underreported bit of history is that the original settlers referred to their little village as "de fuycke" (which of course refers to its shape in relationship to the river). So Albany went from "de fuycke" to the "district of the beaver" or Beverwyck and only thanks to the British takeover in 1664 did we end up with the current name, Albany, which we can't really make fun of unless we make it smaller.

When in Albany...

Here are a few (check the big list for a more complete list):

Places to Eat

Albany Pump Station: 19 Quackenbush Square, Albany, 447-9000. Conveniently located around the corner from the Albany Visitor's Center, the Pump Station has delicious food and a friendly bar. (A large selection of beer is brewed on the premises, which was the 1870s pumping station for the city of Albany.)

Bombers Burrito Bar: 258 Lark Street, Albany, 935-1098. This is Albany's landmark burrito bar. A new location is now open in Schenectady at 447 State Street, 374-3548.

Bros Tacos: 319 Ontario Street, Albany, 935-1098. This is a tiny Mexican place just off Madison with an unusual and wide variety of fresh tacos and burritos. The seafood burrito was a tasty surprise.

Café Capriccio: 49 Grand Street, Albany, 465-0439. Café Capriccio offers gourmet Italian dining at its best. It is cozy and grand at the same time.

Caffe Italia: 662 Central Avenue, 459-8029. For casual dining with absolutely superb food, you must dine here.

Le Canard Enchaine: 25 Quackenbush Square, at the corner of Clinton and Broadway, Albany, 465-1111. A casual and moderately priced French bistro this restaurant offers really tasty appetizers and a prix-fixe menu that is one of the best deals in town.

Debbie's Kitchen: 456 Madison Avenue, Albany, 463-3829. This venue is loved for its superb lunch menu and killer desserts.

Ichiban: 338 Central Avenue, Albany, 432-0358, and 1652 Western Avenue, Albany, 869-9585. Offering both Chinese and Japanese cuisine, everything here is delicious. Their orange tofu dinner is wonderful. Yes, wonderful tofu.

Iron Gate Café: 182 Washington Avenue, Albany, 445-3555. Great sand-wiches at great prices. One of the best places in town to get lunch.

Jack's Oyster House: 42 State Street, Albany, 465-8854. Opened in 1913, Jack's continues to serve excellent seafood and steak in its down-town restaurant. French-American cuisine.

Miss Albany Diner: 893 Broadway, Albany, 465-9148. Look for the giant Nipper. Cozy, and by that we mean small, historic diner, with great break-fasts and lunches. If you are just passing through, this is a must visit.

Melville's Mug: 5 Clinton Square, Albany (across from the Palace Theater), 694-9991. Melville's Mug offers pastries, sandwiches, and Green Moun-tain Coffee. Melville's Mug stays open before Palace Theater events.

Wolffs Biergarten: 895 Broadway, Albany, 427-2461. You can get all kinds of wursts here to go with your German beer. Sit at a picnic table to enjoy them. Very casual setting (there are peanut shells on the floor). You'll feel like you're having an outdoor picnic, only indoors. Open daily for lunch and dinner and brunch on Sundays. It is located right next to the Miss Albany Diner.

Yono's: 25 Chapel Street, Albany, 436-7747 (located in the Hampton Inn). Yono's provides comfortable elegance and the absolute best Indo-nesian and Continental dishes. The restaurant is only open for dinner; and unfortunately it is closed on Sundays.

Places to Shop

Albany Institute of History and Art Gift Shop: 125 Washington Ave-nue, Albany, 463-4478. Most people don't think of the Institute as a shopping destination, but the it houses a large and interesting gift shop stocked with jewelry, books, art, collectibles, and a whole lot more. It is easy to find a great gift here.

Dove and Hudson: 296 Hudson (corner of Dove and Hudson), Albany, 432-4518. The BEST used book store we have ever been to. The quality and range shows that the books here have been carefully selected and not just collected to take up shelf space. If you read, you should get to know this place.

Earthworld: 537 Central Avenue, Albany, 459-2400. This is Albany's best comic book store with an annual Free Comic Book Day every May.

Elissa Halloran Designs: 225 Lark Street, Albany, 432-7090. Offering original jewelry, artful gifts, and accessories, this is one of the few places to purchase a classy gift in the downtown area.

Lodge's: 75 North Pearl Street, Albany, 463-4646. Albany's oldest store, Lodge's sells clothing for the whole family and is a place to find things you didn't know were still being made.

Opus Igor: 260 Lark Street, Albany, 396-5360. This shop carries consignment clothing and original work by local craftspeople.

Romeo's: 299 Lark Street, Albany, 434-4014. Gifts, cards, home décor, and more can be purchased at their upstairs shop.

Treasure Chest Thrift Shop: 295 Hamilton Street, Albany, 436-7451. Two floors of house wares, books, clothing, and furniture are on sale, with proceeds supporting the Damien Center (a community outreach center for people living with and affected by HIV/AIDS). This shop usually has one of the more interesting collections of merchandise.

Silver Birch Trading Post: 294 Delaware Avenue, Albany, 439-0724. Silver Birch is a nice art and gift store located near the Spectrum Theater. A lot of local art is displayed here.

Going Green in Albany

When we first looked into the greening of Albany, we found a Web site listing all of the recycling options for local businesses, including composting their food waste and a whole lot of other things that sounded great. Then we realized we were reading about Albany, California. Albany, New York is another story. Once a week, the city will pick up the regular glass bottles, metal, paper, and cardboard for recycling if you live in an apartment building with four or less units. The Department of General Services manages a large composting area at the end of Erie Boulevard, which has piles of free mulch if you need to pick up a bucket or two for your garden. The Governor's Mansion is heading in a greener direction as are some new companies, but if you want them to really work at it, you'll have to push your Congressional representative. In the mean time, what can you do as an individual? Here are a few ideas.

1. Try bicycling to work. We know it is very hard to find safe passage on most roads, but in the summer months when there is less school bus and car traffic, it is an option you might try a few days a week.

2. Do your laundry in cold water. We weren't really sure about this for all of our wash, but we tried the Tide

made for cold water and the clothes really did come out clean and smelled nice, too. Each large load washed in cold water saves about $1 worth of electricity.

3. Hang your clothes on a line or drying rack. Dryers use a lot of electricity. If you need that soft fluff or a way to remove all of the cat hair that doesn't come off in the wash then run your dried wash in the dryer for 10 minutes. Again this saves about $1 a load.

4. If you drink only bottled water, have it delivered in the 5-gallon reusable jugs and fill a thermos (preferably metal or glass-lined) to carry with you. Otherwise, get a Brita or something like it to filter your tap water. This will drastically cut down on those plastic water bottles floating around.

5. When the 30-year-old refrigerator we inherited died, we wanted to have it repaired rather than dump it. However, even if you fix an old fridge it still will eat an enormous amount of electricity compared with the new energy-efficient ones. So, we got a new one, and no kidding, our electric bill dropped more than $75 each month. And the old one was recycled, as well.

6. Eat and buy locally. We know you've heard this over and over, but it makes sense. There are farmers' markets all year round now where you can purchase fresh, organic foods and talk to the people who actually grow it. Read *Animal, Vegetable, Miracle A Year of Food Life* by Barbara Kingsolver. It is wonderful.

7. In keeping with No. 6 join the Community Supported Agriculture (CSA). For a set fee (it's been around $400 a season) at the beginning of a growing season, you buy a "share" of the farmer's production. Each week at a local farmers' market you can then pick up your "share" of what he grows. In the early season, you get what's available, which seems like it's not very much, but when August rolls around, you'll be taking home so many vegetables, you won't know what to do with them. Everyone benefits in this program. The farmer gets financial help getting started for the season and you get fresh, local food. There is a list of vegetable and meat farmers who participate. It can be found by Googling CSA farms.

8. Now if you are not really into *doing* anything, but you can spare $7 month, go to www.newwindenergy.com/ny and join the Community Energy drive to support wind power. You'll still get your electricity from National Grid, but ALL of the extra money goes to support wind or renewable energy in New York. It will just be added to your electric bill.

9. You've heard this one thousands of times: Switch to compact fluorescent bulbs. They consume much less energy, last longer, and once you get used to the half-second delayed start time, they are not much different from the incandescent bulbs. You will still need regular bulbs for any dimmer switches you might have, but use a lower wattage bulb.

10. Think before you use pesticides. Plenty of nontoxic household supplies can do most of the same stuff. Vinegar works better than Roundup on weeds. It also can clean glass and unclog drains better than Drano if you follow it up with boiling water. Check product ingredients. Bonami is one of the cleansers out there with no chlorine and works great for a number of cleaning jobs.

11. Encourage your neighborhood (or the entire city) to have a free exchange day when you all haul out the things you don't need anymore and trade them for something you might need. You know the old saying about one man's garbage being another's treasure. This could help to either clean out your apartment or furnish it.

12. Use re-usable bags. Unless you need the plastic ones to pick up after your dog, just leave a couple of canvas bags in your car or by your door ready to go. Even places like Wal-Mart and Target let you bring in your own bags now.

13. Remove yourself from national mailing lists by sending your name, address, and signature to: Mail Preference Service, c/o Direct Marketing Association, P.O. Box 643, Carmel, NY 10512.

14. Save on your heating bills by turning down the thermostat, at least while you're sleeping, and put on a sweater. There's a product called Seal and Peel caulking that is great for stopping air leaks around windows and doors in the winter. It really does eliminate drafts and is easy

to take off with no residual gunk if you put it on thick enough.

15. Take shorter showers. We know it feels great to stand around in a hot shower but this costs a fortune and wastes water. If you need to take longer showers, install a low-flow showerhead and lower the water temperature to at least 120 degrees. If you have a roommate who takes a 45-minute shower every day, he is costing you about $50 per month in extra gas or electric bills. Really.

Now, we know that just changing light bulbs is not going to make up for the huge imprint emerging manufacturing nations are making on the environment, but we have to do something on an individual level. And although we'd like to think these tips will make a huge difference, they might only make a little one. But at least they will save you a lot of money in the mean time.

Oh Boy, Troy!!!!!

Just north of Albany, on the other side of the river lies Troy. Until 1787, the area was just a farming community, part of the 800,000-acre patroon-ship of Van Rensselaer. In 1787, a small town was laid out and became the "Town of Troy" in 1791. It graduated to a village in 1801 and finally a city, which was chartered in 1816. Troy's name is taken from Homer's Iliad and is one of dozens of classically named towns and cities through-out New York. That makes all of the residents of Troy, Trojans, which is a much cooler sounding name than Ithacans, Uticans, or Syracusians. Like Albany, Troy's location at the end of the deep-water navigational part of the Hudson, along with access to the Erie and Champlain canals, made it a perfect spot for industrial growth. Unlike Albany, and a good thing too, it did not have Gov. Rockefeller dumping the debris from building the Empire State Plaza into its riverfront and putting a high-way on it.

Troy was known around the world for its steel and iron industries. Henry Burden got his start in the iron and steel business of Troy as superintendent of the Troy Iron and Nail factory. He soon took it over and it became H. Burden and Sons, which produced close to 1 million horseshoes a week during the Civil War, effectively putting all of the local blacksmiths out of business. The first American Bessemer Converter was built on the Poestenkill River in 1865.[2] Bell factories popped up across the river in West Troy (Watervliet), including the Meneely Bell Com-pany, which made the replacement for the cracked Liberty Bell in 1876. During Troy's industrial growth period more than 125 trains arrived here each day.

---

[2] A Bessemer converter is something that blasts air through molten iron to get rid of impurities. It was used to make steel at low cost.

In 1825 a local housewife named Hannah Montague, came up with the idea for the detachable collar, which started another major business for Troy. Troy produced 90% of them under the Cluett, Peabody and Co. name. The last Cluett, Peabody factory closed in the 1980s, which was quite a long time after most of the shirt-making businesses headed south.

A number of catastrophic fires throughout its history continually changed the look of Troy; however the last big fire in 1862 really destroyed much of its downtown. It was rebuilt during one of the more attractive architectural eras and has stayed that way. The combination of cheaper southern labor, highways replacing the need for water access, and prohibition, which eliminated thousands of jobs in the area's very large beer-making business, spelled the end for the local economy in Troy. And so, by the late 1950s, growth-wise, Troy fell asleep—which sometimes can be a good thing. In Troy's case, nothing changed in the downtown area. There was no urban renewal and no renovations. Everything from the golden age was left untouched. The movies *Ironweed, Age of Innocence, The Bostonians, Scent of a Woman,* and *The Time Machine* all used Troy's past as their backdrop. Today it appears that Troy's attempts at a comeback are working. Here are some of the places you should visit and things to see when you make the trek to Troy.

Places to Visit in Troy

Riverspark Visitor's Center: 251 River Street, 270-8667. You should stop in here first because they know Troy. They have walking tour maps, guides, local business and event guides, a really good orientation film that is FREE, and they actually have bicycles you can borrow to ride around town. The Visitor's Center is not easy to find, although its sign is on River Street whenever it is open. You have to go downstairs to get to the Visitor's Center, but doing so will make your visit better.

Frear's Troy Cash Bazaar: Corner of Fulton and Third. William Henry Frear began his career as a salesman and businessman extraordinaire in 1859 in Troy at the age of 18. In 1865, he opened his first store in Troy and by 1897 he opened his world famous Frear's Troy Cash Bazaar, which eventually housed more than 53 different stores under one roof. Frear coined the phrase "Satisfaction Guaranteed, or Your Money Cheerfully Refunded." The store closed by the beginning of the 1960s and has been carefully restored for commercial and office use. The original wrought iron and marble staircase, and its glass dome are absolutely gorgeous! You can access the Bazaar during the week by going up to the second floor of the Troy Atrium and going through the doorway over the CVS. You can also go in through the door to the Frear Building on 3rd Street, take the elevator up to the second floor, and get to the staircase that way. Go see it.

Oakwood Cemetery: 186 Oakwood Avenue (Route 40) off Hoosick Street, 272-7520. The cemetery was incorporated in 1848 and approximately 60,000 are people buried there. It is one of the most beautiful cemeteries in the country with more than 400 wooded acres with five lakes, waterfalls, and an unbelievable 100-mile panoramic view of the Hudson River. You can see from the Catskills to the Adirondacks from the bluffs in this cemetery. The Gardner Earl Memorial Chapel and Crematorium alone is worth the visit here. This chapel was built in 1888–1889 by the Earls, who made their fortune in Troy's detachable collar business, as a memorial to their only son Gardner. During a trip to Europe a few years before his death, Gardner became very interested in cremation, which was virtually unheard of in this country. When he died, as per his request, he was cremated in Buffalo, the location of the closest crematory. In his honor, the Earls built the Earl Chapel with the first crematory in eastern New York. The first cremation took place in 1890. Inside there are eight Tiffany windows, marble mosaics, Maitland Armstrong stained glass windows, hand-carved oak and custom bronze work. You can take a virtual tour of this chapel on the Oakwood Cemetery web page. Many famous people are buried here, including "Uncle Sam" Wilson, Emma Willard, and Russell Sage. There is a nice memorial monument for Robert Ross who believed in the vote for all and while poll watching was murdered on election day, March 6, 1894 by a gang of repeat voters (part of the then Democratic machine).

Troy Savings Bank Music Hall: 30 Second Street, 273-0038. Built in 1875 as the headquarters for the now absorbed Troy Savings Bank, the top floor houses an acoustic marvel of a music hall. As good as the sound is, the seats have been as uncomfortable. Even though they added padding to them in the last few years, they are still hard to sit still in. Luckily, most of the concerts will make you forget all about that. Besides the original frescoes, the Odell Opus 190 Organ installed in the music hall in 1890 is up and playing again. The organ was built in 1882 for William Belden, a rich man from Manhattan, who sold it to the music hall in 1889. When Troy slid into its decline of the 1960s, no one had the money or inclination to support the arts and the music hall and its organ fell into disrepair. In 1979, the Troy Savings Bank Revitalization Committee was founded as a not-for-profit organization and they saved the music hall. In 2006, the organ was back in playable condition. In 1989, the Troy Savings Bank Music Hall was named a national historic landmark. The music hall is so cool it even has its own myspace page.

Troy Public Library (aka William Howard Hart Memorial Library): 100 Second Street, 274-7071. Mary E. Hart built the library as a memorial to her husband, William Howard Hart in 1897. Designed by architects J. Stewart Barney and Henry Otis Chapman in the American Renaissance style, this is one spiffy building. However, for all of its grandeur there was never enough money for the library to fully operate. It changed its name to the Troy Public Library in 1903 in hopes of attracting some municipal funding. That never really worked either. Even so, it has managed to stay open as a free public library for more than 100 years. This is the only library in which you will find a Tiffany window over the circulation desk. Frederick Wilson designed the window, which portrays Venetian scholar Aldus Manutius (1450-1515). On the upper right corner of the window is the quote from Isidore of Saville "Study as if you were to live forever and live as if you were to die tomorrow." Sounds like a good idea.

Ilium Building: 400 Fulton Street. Situated next to the Fulton Street Gallery is one of Troy's first skyscrapers, a whole five stories high. Frederick M. Cummings designed the Ilium Building. It has detailed stone work all the way around and a very nice entryway. We were told that its elevator is the oldest in the city. It certainly feels like it when it tries to climb to the upper floors. The Ilium is home to a number of artists with studio space upstairs. Check to see if they're open during one of Troy's Night Out and be amazed.

Russell Sage College and the Magnificent Margaret Olivia Slocum Sage. Russell Sage College was founded in 1916 using the buildings of the once Emma Willard School, which had moved to its new campus up on Pawling Avenue in 1910. The original Emma Willard School was called the Troy Female Seminary and was founded by Emma Willard with the sure knowledge that women were certainly smart enough to learn geography and math just like the boys. One of her students was Margaret Slocum, a suffragist.

Margaret married the wealthy financier Russell Sage when she was in her early 40s; this was his second marriage. He was mean and miserly but very rich and when he died in 1906, Margaret Olivia Slocum Sage inherited upwards of $50 million and started giving it away almost immediately. She put her husband's name on everything from the Russell Sage Foundation, Russell Sage Laboratory at Rensselaer Polytechnic Institute to the Russell Sage College itself. No one is really sure whether she did this as some inside joke that only she knew, or whether it was just another aspect of her generosity. The original college operated under Emma Willard's charter but eventually got its own. It was strictly a women's college offering a liberal arts education. Men were admitted to the Troy campus during World War II only as an emergency measure. In 1949, the Albany campus opened offering men and women 2- and

4-year degrees. This became the Sage Junior College of Albany. The Troy campus houses the amazing New York State Theater Institute (NYSTI), which is located in the Schacht Fine Arts Center.

As well as building the new Emma Willard School and renovating the old one and turning it into the Russell Sage College, Mrs. Sage donated money to Yale University, Cornell University, and piles of it to Rensselaer Polytechnic Institute. The Russell Sage Foundation continues to fund projects that impact social and living conditions throughout the United States. She even bought an island in the Gulf of Mexico as a home for wild birds. WOW!!

Rensselaer Polytechnic Institute (RPI): In his later years, Stephen Van Rensselaer, the last patroon of Albany, established the Rensselaer School (RPI) in 1824 "for the purpose of instructing persons, who may choose to apply themselves, in the application of science to the common purposes of life." He co-founded the school with Amos Eaton who became its first senior professor. (Eaton had an unbelievably tragic life up to this point including being sent to prison at hard labor for life after he was framed for forgery during the very hectic and shady land dealing time of the Erie Canal construction. Gov. DeWitt Clinton pardoned him unconditionally when they found the evidence against him had been false.) At Rensselaer, women were also admitted, in courses of study that prepared them for a teaching career. Eight actually graduated in 1835. If you wanted to learn science, Emma Willard's Troy Female Seminary was just down the hill, and there Eaton taught science to the women (including Emma Willard herself).

RPI began in the building housing Troy's first bank, the Farmer's Bank, which was built in 1801. The building housed classrooms, laboratories, a library, living space for students, and even an observatory. The school stayed in this building until 1844 when the property was claimed as part of the Amos Eaton estate (Eaton died in 1842). In 1834, the Van der Heyden (founder of Troy) mansion also became part of RPI. After being bumped from the bank, the city of Troy turned over property known as the Infant School at State and 6th to RPI and RPI stayed there until it was destroyed during the great fire of 1862. After this point, RPI started to get serious and built its own building called the Main Building in 1864. Alas, fire took this one as well in 1904, and the property was turned over to Troy. In 1907, The Approach, that massive granite staircase you can see looking up to the campus from downtown, was completed. In 1906, after Russell Sage's death (see above), Mrs. Sage donated $1 million for the construction of the Russell Sage Laboratory. The campus has continually grown, building new buildings and absorbing old ones, including the purportedly haunted West Hall built in 1868, which was the Troy Hospital built to aid Irish cholera victims. The new EMPAC (Experimental Media and Performing Arts Center) opened October 3, 2008.

The Hirsch Observatory on campus opens its view to the universe free to the public on Saturdays from 8 to 10 p.m. between February and mid-November. RPI is one of the oldest engineering schools in North America. George W.G. Ferris (of the Ferris wheel) graduated from RPI in 1881.

Troy's Antique District: River Street, as well as many other location around Troy. There are quite a few antique stores all within walking distance of each other and whether you're looking for fancy antiques or funky kitsch, you might be able to find it in Troy. We have found some really weird and wonderful items in a number of the stores. If you are lazy, and looking for one-stop shopping, start with the Bournebrook Antique Center located at 172 River Street (273-3027). This is a multid-ealer two-floor delight with a full range of furniture of all styles, jewelry, art, china, and collectibles. When you are done here, head down to River Street for a number of smaller, interesting antique shops, the River Rocks Bead shop, and the fabulous Beat Shop for old records. There are a few good vintage shops for retro furniture and clothing further down on River Street and if you hop over to 4th you'll find Twilight, which sells vintage clothing. Bournebrook will keep to its regular hours but some of the smaller shops have a much looser idea of business hours. Call to be sure of them, but make the trip, it's worth it.

The Troy Waterfront Farmer's Market: 312-5749 (year-round). From November to April, it is located at the Uncle Sam Atrium from 9 a.m. to 1 p.m. From May to October, it is in Troy's Riverfront Park along Front Street in Troy, also from 9 a.m. to 1 p.m. What can we say? This is the best farmer's market around. You can find fresh produce year-round from local farmers, as well as fresh cheeses, baked goods and nonhomogenized farm fresh milk in glass bottles from Gumaer Dairy. There is always music, hot food and hot fair-traded coffee. You can find local wines, honey, art, and fresh pesto. Make this part of your Saturday routine. It will make your life better.

Burden Ironworks Museum: 1 East Industrial Parkway, Troy, 274-5267. Housed in the old brick offices of the Burden Iron Works, the museum is open by appointment only. It houses artifacts and information from Troy's industrial past. Burden was known for its massive horseshoe production during the Civil War, but earlier, it was the invention of his Burden Spike Machine patented in 1839, which could make a complete spike with head and point, that helped build the railroads of America. For tours and information, visit www.hudsonmohawkgateway.org

Watervliet Arsenal–and Museum: 1 Buffington Street, Watervliet, 266-5111. The Watervliet Arsenal is the oldest, continually running arsenal in the United States and is still producing much of the artillery for the army. It was built in 1813 to support the War of 1812 on a 12-acre site along the Hudson River. It now covers 142 acres and includes the Benet Laboratories. In 1887, it became known as America's cannon factory, and cannons remain its principle product. In 1988, it opened up the grounds for its 175th anniversary and you could see the old living quarters and the beautiful greenhouse built in 1903. It has a wonderful museum housed in the "Iron Building," a cast iron building erected in 1859 to store equipment. The free "Big Guns" exhibit is open to the public 10 a.m. to 3 p.m., Sunday through Thursday.

Did You Know?

That on Fourth Street in Troy there is a fencing school. It's not your namby-pamby foil and epee fencing school. We are talking sabers here, and we are talking nationally ranked sword smiths. Go to beachesny.net

When in Troy . . .

Park in the Atrium Garage off Third Street.

Where to Eat

Troy offers a full range of eating choices from cheap and good to elegant and pricey. Here are some places to eat if you are visiting.

Ali Baba: 2243 15th Street, Troy, 273-1170. Offering Turkish cuisine, everything we have tried here is delicious and the lavash bread with yogurt is irresistible.

Baby Badass: 409 Fulton Street, Troy, 268-1788. A great little M-F takeout lunch place with a one price menu. The original Badass Burrito is still at 443 Fifth Street in Lansingburgh.

Brown's Brewing Co.: 417 River Street, Troy, 273-2337. The pub fare is good, but as the name suggests, this also is a great (award-winning) brewery with a beautiful river view.

Bruegger's Bagels: 55 Congress Street, Troy, 274-4469. For a light breakfast or lunch, Bruegger's has the best bagels on Earth and this store is where it all started.

The Daily Grind: 46 Third Street, Troy, 272-8658. This is a homey coffee place with soups, sandwiches, and baked goods. It provides comfortable and relaxing seating areas and a great open mic on Thursday nights.

De Fazio's Pizzeria: 266 Fourth Street, Troy, 271-1111. This is where to get that wood-fired pizza you have been craving. There are 21 gourmet varieties, all so good you won't be able to resist eating a slice before you get back to your car. You can eat in, take out, or have it delivered. Their deli, again, all good, is located next door.

Flavour Café and Lounge: 228 Fourth Street, Troy, 266-9253. Located in Troy's little, Little Italy, Flavour has more than the 31 varieties of coffee advertised on its sign, as well as also a number of teas, soups, salads, wraps, desserts, and Wi-Fi.

Holmes & Watson: 450 Broadway, Troy, 273-8526. This is a good choice for lunch or dinner as the restaurant offers a large sandwich menu and more than 100 choices of beer and ale (25 beers on draft).

Lo Porto's Ristorante Caffe: 85 Fourth Street, Troy, 273-8546. The food is amazing and abundant. We love it here. Lunch is a great deal, but for the amount of food you get for dinner the prices are more than reasonable. The calamari appetizer is enough to feed a small country.

Marmora Café: 203 River Street, Troy, 266-9300. You'll find Egyptian specialties here. Stop by on Troy Night Out for a generous and really good gyros.

Muza: 1300 15th Street (near Congress), Troy, 271-6892. Excellent family style Polish/Eastern European cuisine. When we were deciding what to order, the waitress told us that we really wanted stuffed cabbage, and she was right.

River Street Café: 429 River Street, Troy, 273-2740. Delicious fresh food is served in a beautiful setting with a great view of the river.

Shalimar: 407 Fulton Street, Troy, 273-8744. Delicious Indian fare with a very nice lunch buffet at a good price.

Spill'n the Beans: 13 Third Street, Troy, 268-1028. With a large selection of coffee, eclectic breakfast and lunch selections, and better-than-most pastries, this place has an extremely comfortable lounge area with a fireplace so you can really sit and enjoy your coffee.

Tosca Grille: 200 Broadway, Troy, 272-3013. This place oozes grandeur and the food never disappoints. This is an upscale restaurant that we reserve for special occasions.

*Special Note: **Dinosaur Bar-B-Que** of Syracuse is opening in Troy some time in late spring 2010 at 377 River Street. Their ribs are FABULOUS! We can't wait.

Places to Shop

Troy has a varied collection of stores, most within walking distance of each other and when they are open, you can fill hours just browsing through them. We especially like these.

Aquilonia Comics: 412 Fulton Street, Troy, 271-1069. If you are a comic book or graphic novel collector then you already live here, but if you are a novice collector this is the place to get your feet wet.

Bournebrook Antique Center: 172 River Street, Troy, 273-3027. These guys keep the most regular hours and have a huge selection of all kinds of stuff, including a good collection of antique jewelry from assorted vendors.

The Broken Mold Studio: 284 River Street, Troy, 273-6041. Here you can find handcrafted pottery and sign up for pottery lessons as well. Visit thebrokenmoldstudio.com for a schedule of classes.

Cathedral Music: 1813 Fifth Avenue, Troy, Troy, 273-5138. Handcrafted guitars by a number of expert builders are the highlight here. Made from exotic wood, each is an absolute work of art.

The Counties of Ireland: 77 Third Street, Troy, 687-0054. Yes, this store sells stuff from Ireland, including gorgeous sweaters, scarves, and jewelry, teas, cookies, and a variety of other Irish gifts.

Living Room: 274 River Street, Troy, 266-9311. Living Room features a good selection of antique and retro furnishings. Antiek (their sign says Antiques Warehouse) at 78 Fourth Street, across from Lo Porto's, 272-3160, is owned by the same family and has a bigger selection of mostly furniture.

Market Block Books: 290 River Street, Troy, 328-0045. An independent bookstore, this store offers a great selection of books and a comfortable browsing atmosphere.

Martinez Gallery: 3 Broadway, Troy, 274-9377. This is another of the galleries in Troy we like a lot. The gallery focuses mostly on Latino and Latin American art and every show is exciting. If you are not able to afford one of the installed pieces, the gallery has a nice group of prints and unframed pieces that are definitely affordable.

The Paper Sparrow: 288 River Street, Troy, 272-7227. Funky local and imported jewelry, clothing (baby stuff too), bags, local art, and a lot more are the features here. There are changing exhibits in the back room.

The River Street Beat Shop: 197 River Street, Troy, 272-0433. A great selection of vinyl, DVDs, and tapes, with low prices on everything.

Romanation Jewelers: 48 Third Street, Troy, 272-0643. Since 1952, Romanation has been selling fine jewelry and watches. The store carries a good selection of vintage jewelry, as well.

The Spinning Seed: 272 River Street, Troy, 268-1499. This is a store good for you and the planet, selling organic and fair-traded clothing, food, and gifts for you and your pet.

Truly Rhe: 11 Second Street, Troy, 424-5303. A relatively new addition to Troy, Rhe's is a beautiful store filled with a timeless collection of women's clothing and accessories. Rhe's also has a rack of lightly used designer clothing in the back.

Vintage Options: 205 River Street, Troy, 272-2083. A real blast from the past offering an ever-changing selection of retro clothing and accessories. The store is shared with Odyssey Art and Antiques (271-3888), which has just what their name implies.

A Brief Look at Schenectady

Our Own City of Lights

It's not like you can stroll across to Schenectady from Albany but the King's Highway (Albany calls it Central Avenue, Schenectady calls it State nowadays), will still connect the two formerly stockaded cities. The name is taken from the Mohawk Indians meaning, "land near the pine barrens."

A group led by Arendt Van Curler first settled Schenectady in 1661. Tired of living the patroonship lifestyle, Van Curler petitioned Gov. Stuyvesant to allow him to purchase land from the Mohawks so that they could actually own the land they worked on. The group got the go-ahead and divided up their Schenectady into nice little plots and homes. The population grew to approximately 400 people before it all ended in 1690.

On February 8, 1690, a group of French and their Indian allies came down from Canada and attacked a sleeping and unguarded stockade. Fire was set to almost all of the homes and as their inhabitants ran outside, they were slaughtered. One settler managed to escape, and although wounded, he rode the 5 hours to Albany for help. When he returned with help the following morning, the village was nothing but burning embers surrounded by the dead bodies of 60 men, women, and children lying in the snow. Only two of the attackers were killed in the battle. The Albany militia followed them back north and killed 17 more. After such a blow, it seemed difficult to imagine that the town could come back. After 30 years, the population only grew back to about one-third of what it was. But the Dutch carried on.

In 1765, Schenectady became a borough and in 1798 it was chartered as the city of Schenectady. Around 1779, the locals thought it was time to think about building an institution for higher learning and in January 1792 the citizens of Albany actually started saving money to build a college (they thought somewhere in Albany would be nice). The college turned out to be Union College and it was built in Schenectady (Union was founded in 1795).

In the early 1800s, the Watervliet Shakers introduced broomcorn to the Schenectady area. It adapted well to the soil and became a major crop and broom-making a major industry. Schenectady became known as the broom capital of the world. There were more than a dozen broom manufacturers in Glenville alone. By the middle of the 19th century, The Schenectady Locomotive Works had its beginnings and by the 1860s turned out five to six locomotives per month.

Growth was helped by the proximity to the river and the Erie Canal, but really took off when in 1887 Thomas Edison moved his Edison Machine Works here. In 1892, the company became General Electric (GE). George Westinghouse invented his rotary engine and air brakes in Schenectady. The American Locomotive Works (ALCO) formed in 1901 by merging a number of smaller companies, including the Schenectady Locomotive Works, and made almost every steam and diesel locomotive that crossed America. (GE pretty much put ALCO out of business with its own diesel-electric locomotives in 1969). GE still builds locomotives among millions of other things and today is still one of the largest companies in the world. In the past, GE was the largest employer in Schenectady, but today, not so much.

Schenectady was called "The City That Lights and Hauls the World." Although that doesn't quite roll off the tongue, it did describe the city.

Places You Should Visit

Proctor's Theater: 432 State Street, Schenectady, 346-6204. Frederick Francis Proctor opened this theater on Dec.27, 1926 to rave reviews. The 2,700-seat theater was opulent and state of the art. Sound was installed for the talkies in 1928 and the first public unveiling of television was here in 1930. The theater did well throughout the 1940s but then things turned south and eventually Proctor's was closed and taken by the city for back taxes. With its future facing a wrecking ball, in 1979 a group of concerned citizens bought Proctor's from the city for $1 and revitalized the theater. In 2003, a $30 million expansion/renovation was begun and today a magnificent new/old Proctor's brings Broadway to upstate. The GE Theater and the smaller Upstairs@440 complete a top-notch performing arts complex. And if that's not enough, there's a great farmer's market here on Sundays.

Mabee Farm Historic Site: 1080 Main Street, Rotterdam Junction, 887-5073. Mabee Farm is the oldest house in the Mohawk Valley, dating back to the late 1600s. The grounds include the house, barns, the Mabee family cemetery, and beautiful gardens all of which is open to the public. The site is owned by the Schenectady County Historical Society (374-0263) and hosts numerous festivals and events during the year.

The Stockade Historic District: Bounded by Union Street on the south, the Mohawk River on the north, the Binne Kill on the west, and the railroad tracks on the east, the Stockade District is the first named historic district in New York State. It has more than 40 homes that are older than 200 years and some date even farther back than that. This is the area that came back after the massacre of 1690, which nearly wiped out Schenectady. As Schenectady grew, businesses were growing and the Stockade District had a number of commercial buildings mixed in with the houses. In 1819, fire wiped out more than 200 structures here, mostly commercial. This fire turned out to be a good thing for the neighborhood because when the businesses rebuilt, they moved down to State Street to be closer to the coming Erie Canal. This left the area mostly residential. There are a number of architectural styles represented here, but it's really nice to see the old Dutch high-gabled roofs all in a row. You get a great view of these coming into Schenectady by train. The neighborhood started to decline around the 1950s, but after the first few people came in to renovate what they saw as a place with great possibilities, more followed. They formed The Stockade Association in 1962 to start to preserve the beauty and history of the area. The Stockade Association hosts its annual art show, usually the weekend after Labor Day.

Liberty Park: Corner of State and Washington, across from Schenectady County Community College. Back in the 1950s, to commemorate their 40th anniversary, the Boy Scouts decided to erect replicas of the Statue of Liberty across America. There are more than 200 of these 8.5-foot copper replicas spread throughout 39 states and New York has 6 of them, one located in Schenectady. The park also has the last of the historic iron signs welcoming you to Schenectady and commemorating the massacre of 1690.

Union College: 807 Union Street, Schenectady. In 1779, people started to talk about building a place for higher education in the tri-city area. By 1792, they actually started to raise money for this undertaking and by 1795, Union College was founded, its first location being in the Stockade District. Union was the first college chartered by the Regents of the State of New York. It wasn't until 1814 that it moved to its present 100-acre location off Union Street. Eliphalet Nott was president of the college from 1804 to 1866. Under his long tenure, the college experienced tremendous growth and a period of deep decline. Nott came up with a novel lottery system to raise money for the school, but his questionable practice of mixing college finances with his own, brought him and the college under investigation by the Senate. Although cleared of any wrongdoing, the scandal put Union College into a 25-year tailspin, and at its lowest point in 1888, the college lost about 75% of its enrollment. In 1894, Mr. Raymond took the helm as president. He focused on science and added a Department of Electrical Engineering and Applied Physics. He brought the brilliant (and wickedly funny) scientist Charles Steinmetz from GE to head the department. (Steinmetz gave us alternating current [A/C] power.) The college was back on track.

Union has a beautiful campus, the centerpiece of which is the Nott Memorial, a 16-sided, mosaic-topped building built in 1875. The second floor is home to the Mandeville Gallery, which is always worth visiting. U.S. president, Chester A. Arthur, graduated from Union in 1848.

GE Realty Plots: East of Union College, off Nott Street. In 1899, Union College was looking for a way to eliminate some of its debt and decided to sell off a 75-acre parcel of land east of the campus known as "College Woods." At the same time, GE was looking for a place to build a residential neighborhood for its scientists and executives. So in a win–win situation, Union paid off its debt with GE's $57,000 purchase of the 75 acres. The realty plots were designed by Parse and DeForrest with a plan to make a very park-like neighborhood consisting of curving roads, well-landscaped, large lots, and very grand single-family homes costing a minimum of $4,000 each (twice the going rate in 1900). Today, the realty plots cover about 90 acres and contain about 100 homes built between 1900 and 1927. Driving through the neighborhood, with its stream crossed by stone-arched bridges and the Victorian street names, such as Lennox, Wendell, and Stratford, really takes you back to a much grander time from Schenectady's past. Walking tour maps for the plots are available from the Visitor's Center in the Schenectady Museum on Nott Terrace Heights.

Schenectady Museum and Suit-Bueche Planetarium: 15 Nott Terrace Heights, 382-7890. This is a great little museum that provides a glimpse of some of the innovations that came out of this area. It is a good museum for kids and includes some hands-on learning. The planetarium was completely overhauled in the past few years and has regular programming that will connect you to the stars. The Schenectady Heritage Area Visitor's Center is located here, too, but only has a couple of pamphlets. It does have the walking tour map for the GE realty plots.

When in Schenectady . . .

Places to Eat

This is a short list. For more Schenectady listings, check our BIG List of Eating Out.

Ambition Café: 154 Jay Street, Schenectady, 382-9277. You can get a great sandwich for lunch or dinner here, along with offerings from their full bar. The café features a funky atmosphere and is owned by the same owners as Skinny & Sweet, which is located next door at 156 Jay (377-7990) and sells gifts and goodies.

Bangkok Thai Bistro: 268 State Street, Schenectady, 374-3048. A super-attentive and friendly staff, Bangkok Thai offers a delicious array of Thai dishes. If you are having drinks from their large martini menu, try some of the satisfying appetizers with them.

Chez Daisie Creperie: 183 Jay Street, Schenectady, 344-7082. All kinds of dessert and entrée crepes, as well as wonderful sandwiches that are prepared on artisan bread, can be purchased in this restaurant's cozy French-like setting.

Cornell's Restaurant: 39 N. Jay Street, Schenectady, 370-3825. Cornell's has been located in Schenectady's Little Italy since 1943, and serves up an outstanding menu your Italian grandmother would be jealous of. Go and eat.

Gershon's Deli & Caterers: 1600 Union Street, Schenectady, 393-0617. A mainstay on Union forever this is one of the best real delis around. You can even pick up a loaf of Perreca's wonderful bread here.

Glen Sanders Mansion: 1 Glen Ave., Scotia, 374-7262. This is a great place for an elegant meal in a beautiful setting, with a patio that overlooks the Mohawk River.

Jumpin' Jacks Drive-In: 5 Schonowee Avenue, Scotia (right over the bridge from Schenectady), 393-6101. A seasonal place, Jumpin' Jacks has been around forever serving up great fast food (especially the onion rings) and creamy soft-serve ice cream you can eat while overlooking the beautiful Mohawk River. The U.S. Water Ski Show Team has its home just behind Jack's and you can watch them practice while eating your ice cream. Google U.S. Water Ski Show Team for their show times. This is a summertime must.

Moon and River Café: 115 S Ferry Street, Schenectady, 382-1938. This little café in the middle of the Stockade District offers vegetarian, lighter fare with an eclectic mix of music and performance during their open mics.

Parisi's Steakhouse: 11 N. Broadway, Schenectady, 374-0100. Theater friends of ours love this place at the end of a run for eating well and relaxing.

The Parker Inn: 434 State Street, Schenectady, 688-1001. Parker Inn is the small hotel next to Proctor's and its bar is consistently voted the best hotel bar around. The light fare is tasty and on big Proctor's nights the inn offers a buffet meal.

Peter Pause Restaurant: 535 Nott Street, Schenectady, 382-9278. This is a small, homestyle Italian restaurant. It serves breakfast and lunch and is open from 6 a.m. to 2 p.m.

Pizza King: 124 Jay Street, Schenectady, 347-1234. One of our family's favorite places for great pizzas with unusual toppings. All are delish! Long live the king!

Scotti's Restaurant: 1730 Union Street, Schenectady, 393-7440. One of the best neighborhood Italian restaurants in the area, Scotti's offers a friendly atmosphere, an affordable menu, and a pizza that tastes close to a real New York-style pizza.

Winedown Lounge: 613 Union Street, Schenectady, 344-7086, 344-7039. Although a nice place for after-work drinks the lovely atmosphere and wonderful menu will make want to stay.

A Little Shopping List

For more places to shop in Schenectady see our BIG shopping list.

Hermie's: 727 State Street, Schenectady, 374-7433. A music store run by and for musicians, Hermie's offers a great selection of new and used instruments, as well as expert advice and repairs.

Van Curler Music: 432 State Street, Schenectady (no. 107), 374-5318. Located in the Proctor's Theater Arcade, you can purchase sheet music (your source for NYSSMA), writing supplies, and music gifts.

Open Door Bookstore: 128 Jay Street, Schenectady, 346-2719. Offering a diverse selection of books for all ages in a welcoming atmosphere, you can also find a really nice gallery of quality gifts and toys.

Orion Boutique: 169 Jay Street, Schenectady, 346-4902. This store features imported cigars, a large selection of tobaccos, cigarettes, and all types of pipes.

Perreca's Bakery: 33 N. Jay Street, Schenectady, 372-1875. Perreca's has the best Italian bread in the area—no kidding.

Tough Traveler: 1012 State Street, Schenectady, 377-8526; factory store 393-0168. Tough Traveler has been making its quality luggage, backpacks, kid and dog carriers, and other gear in the area since 1970. When you buy from them, you are getting quality while supporting the local economy at the same time.

Schenectady Museum Gift Store: 15 Nott Terrace Heights, 382-7890, in the museum. Most people overlook museum gift stores, but in this area some of the best sources for great, local gifts are at this museum's store. This one is one of the best, with local art and designer crafts, among other really cute science museum merchandise.

Did You Know?

That Albany was Schenectady before Schenectady was. It was once known as Schau-naugh-ta-da, the land across the pine plains, by the native tribes along the Mohawk. The folk of Fort Orange threw it back to them, by calling the land across the pine plains from Fort Orange (Albany's first incarnation) Schau-naugh-ta-da, now Schenectady.

Of Billiards and Beer

Behind the 8 Ball

Until 1976, Albany was home to the Albany Billiard Ball Company. The factory used to be located at 517 Delaware Avenue and was one of the oldest and largest manufacturers of billiard balls in the world. It is now an A. strip mall or B. a parking lot. If you guessed A., then you are correct. In 1977 it became the Albany-Hyatt Billiard Ball Co., left town, and by 1986 it was gone. Its history is interesting, however, and goes back to the invention of celluloid, the first plastic.

In 1862, a Mr. Parkes of England discovered you could make molded material from a cellulose-based nitrate by adding different solvents. He made all kinds of things, including combs, fishing spools, little plastic Jesus heads, AND billiard balls. However, his Parkesine, although very exciting, was flammable and his business plans were not well thought out. By 1868, his business venture into plastics was over.

Enter John Wesley Hyatt, a young Albanian with a very inventive mind. Around this time, the Phelan and Collender Co. (now Brunswick), maker of billiard tables, offered a $10,000 prize to anyone who could come up with a replacement material for the ivory that was used in making billiard balls. (Just to supply the billiard balls to the United Kingdom in 1860 required the slaughter of 12,000 elephants.) The money was incentive enough for John Wesley and his brother Isaiah to start some serious experimentation. The story goes that he won the competition and never received the prize, but that story is not quite accurate. He had patented a material he called celluloid in 1865. In 1868, he made a billiard ball with a fibrous pulp center and collodion (nitrocellulose) coating for the competition. One problem to remember here, is that this stuff was flammable, and when you get a couple of billiard balls smacking into each other, there is a good chance of an explosion. Probably not quite what the Phelan and Collender Co. was looking for in a billiard ball.

Hyatt kept experimenting and by a chance, he found that by adding camphor, the bursting into flame part was solved. He started the Hyatt Billiard Ball Company in 1868, with the flammable balls, but in 1870 his formulation with the added camphor was patented and he started using that formulation. Pheww! What Hyatt had over Parkes were his designs for the industrial machinery needed to mass-produce good-quality plastic items at a reasonable cost. Not only did he start up the soon-to-be called Albany Billiard Ball Company, but at the same time, he started the Albany Dental Plate Company, which became the Celluloid Manufacturing Company, which moved to Newark, New Jersey in 1873.

The Albany Billiard Ball Company received patents through the 1970s for different formulas for billiard balls. One reason for the company's decline was worldwide competition. After World War II, tariffs on imported billiard balls were lowered from 50% to 20% to increase trade. Albany Billiard's share of the U.S. market dropped to one-third after dominating it for almost a century. John Wesley Hyatt died in New Jersey in 1920.

Science 101

Since celluloid was "invented" in Albany maybe you would like to know what it is. Celluloid is a name given to a material made from nitrocellulose by Hyatt in the early 1860s. He patented a process of combining nitrocellulose with camphor in 1865 to make a variety of plastic items, including billiard balls, dentures, shirt collars, knife handles, and eventually film. The Albany Billiard Ball Company he founded was the largest producer of billiard balls in the world until the late 1970s. Cellulose is the structural component of the cell walls of plants, the most common organic compound on earth. A nitrate is a salt of nitric acid, commonly found in nature (NO_3) and absorbed by plants to make protein. By "nitrating" cellulose you get an explosive material: flash paper, gunpowder, and the like. Henri Braconnot discovered its explosive properties in 1832. Later, it seems by accident, it was observed that you could get a plastic-like material by mixing it with different solvents. However, you still had a very flammable or explosive product. Acetone was one of the earlier solvents used to make the plastic substance, but Hyatt improved the early plastics by using camphor instead, which made a much more stable product. It still was highly flammable and in the case of film, it also yellowed and degraded easily. Safety film with an acetate base replaced this. Today, celluloid has been replaced with other nonflammable plastics, but still is used in guitar picks and ping pong balls.

Beer Here

First a little history. Beer used to be a dark, cloudy, drink for everyman. Beer was a food staple and to keep it on the table, early colonists imported malted barley from Europe and brewed beer at home, as well as importing ale from England. The Gansevoort family was making beer here as early as 1660 and Arendt Van Curler opened his brewery in 1661. As the politics changed, colonists wanted less and less to do with England and that included passing up on the English ale. The problem with beer (before bottle caps and cans) is that it just didn't keep. Rum and later whiskey were easy to make as well, and would keep forever, so colonists started making and drinking the hard stuff. Well before the temperance movement got its start, people started to feel that encouraging beer drinking over hard alcohol would be much better for everyone's health. Mmmm hmmm. And then something happened. Around 1842, in Austria, a method of beer making called lagering could give you a clear, golden brew that became all the rage. It was cold and more refreshing than regular beer.

As immigrants from Europe, especially Germany, were pouring in to America, the craving for this kind of beer was enormous. Breweries popped up everywhere. We have run across at least 13 different companies that used to operate in Albany around 1850. It turns out that to make a really nice lager, you need to store or lager it for months in a cool place. The basement of the local breweries, deep in the clay soil of Albany, proved a perfect storage area for the lagering of beer. The beer business here was *big* business and employed a lot of the local population.

Unfortunately for them, on January 16, 1920, prohibition went into effect and knocked out most of the breweries and the jobs that went with them. (The Albany pharmacists did well dispensing "medicinal" alcohol in alarming quantities.) A few got through the next 13 years by making a near beer (less than 0.5% alcohol) or soft drinks. Those that closed in 1920 included the Hinckel Brewery Co. (AKA Cataract Brewery) 1857–1920 and Quinn & Nolan Ale Brewing Co. 1884–1920 (Quinn and Nolan began as James Quinn, Ale Brewery in 1845). The

Albany Brewing Co., (this was formerly the Arch Street Brewery, which was established in 1796 by Robert Boyd) was reportedly padlocked in 1926.

The Hinckel Brewery building still stands, overlooking Lincoln Park and is currently apartments. If you've always wanted to live in a brewery check it out. The Amsdell Brothers were here from 1851 to 1892 when they decided to move the business to Manhattan. Their building, located on Dove between Jay and Lancaster, still stands: the Knickerbocker apartments. John Taylor's Sons was the largest brewery in the United States in 1860 (founded in 1822 and covering 2 acres between Broadway and the river near Ferry), but by 1903 it had passed out of the family's hands.

Survivors of prohibition included Hedrick Brewing Company, known as the political beer—the company was owned by the Democratic machine boss Dan O'Connell who made sure every bar in Albany, and we mean every, only sold Hedrick draft. Hedrick's stayed in business until 1966. Beverwyck Brewing Company—"Beverwyck, Best Beer Brewed"—opened in 1878, managed to get through prohibition by making nonalcoholic beverages, only to be bought by Schaefer in 1950 and put out of business in 1972. The John S. Dobler Brewing Co., Dobler Lager & Ale, opened in 1865 on Myrtle Avenue and stayed in business until construction of the Empire State Plaza, which took down the neighborhood it was part of around 1960. Dobler mansion was built at the corner of Elm and South Swan streets near the brewery, but was razed during the construction of Rockefeller's concrete monument.

Today, although there isn't a brewery on every corner, we have the very fine C.H. Evans Brewing Co., at the Albany Pump Station in Albany and the ever-popular Brown's Brewery in Troy. Both have some mighty fine brews.

Did You Know?

Legs Diamond, notorious gangster of Albany's prohibition era, was shot on three different occasions before he finally died of multiple gunshot wounds to the back of the head on Dove Street in Albany. His brother Eddie, living a similar lifestyle in Arizona and Colorado (he moved there for his health), was also shot a number of times—once he was ambushed by a rival gang and shot at more than 100 times with no injuries—before he finally checked out.

Some Famous Albanians You Should Know

Albany has quite a few notable people, but here are brief biographies of some of our favorites.

One Awesome Angelica

Angelica Schuyler Church

Angelica Schuyler Church was born February 22, 1756, a scant 5 months after her parents' (Philip Schuyler and Catherine Van Rensselaer) marriage. She was the first of the 11 (8 having survived) children born to the couple. Not only was she born into great wealth and position, she was apparently intelligent and beautiful as well. Which is why we can't imagine what she saw in John Barker Carter, an English gambler on the lam for killing someone during a duel back home. But there was something, and on June 23, 1777 she eloped with him. Can you say scandal? John Barker Carter made his money in various ventures in the all-new United States and late in 1783 changed his named to John Barker

Church. Now, had she not been so impulsive, she would have been free when Alexander Hamilton showed up and stole her heart. As it turned out, Angelica's sister Elizabeth, too, was smitten by Alexander and it was Elizabeth who married Hamilton in December 1780. Some suggest that an affair between Angelica and Hamilton began almost as soon as they met, but she was pregnant at that point with the first of her four children. When she did spend time in America, it was at her town home in the city and there, Angelica, not her sister accompanied Hamilton around New York. Elizabeth was usually safely ensconced in upstate New York, pregnant with one of her eight children.

Church's business dealings brought Angelica back and forth from America to Europe and she was quite happy to be part of the "in" crowd of London and Paris. It was in Paris in 1788 where she first met Thomas Jefferson, who joined the club of Angelica admirers. He fell fast and hard, but it is doubtful whether this relationship went where he wanted it to. His letters to Angelica are owned by the University of Virginia and in one sent in 1789, he suggests they go on a vacation in America and perhaps begin an affair much like the lovers Yoric and Piedmontese from a very popular romance novel of the day. He also suggests a trip to Niagara Falls, which even back in the 1780s was a hot spot for lovers. He kept trying for 10 years.

Aaron Burr, or one of his close associates, figures in a number of events in the Hamilton, Church, and Schuyler families. John Church, himself was in a duel with Burr over a slanderous (but warranted remark) about Burr. Church proved the better shot, but no one was hurt. In 1801, a Burr associate killed Hamilton's son Philip in front of his cousin Philip Church (Angelica's son) in a duel. Three years later, in the same spot with the same pistols, Burr would fire the shot that would kill Alexander Hamilton. The pistols in both fatal duels were those belonging to Angelica's husband, John Barker Church. As he lay dying, Angelica stayed by Hamilton's bed side. She died 10 years later at age 58 and is buried near him in Trinity Church. John Church died in London in 1814. Elizabeth Schuyler Hamilton died at 97, 50 years after her husband's death, and is buried with Hamilton near her sister at Trinity Church.

There is no doubt Hamilton dearly loved his wife—when she died, she was still wearing Hamilton's last letter folded into a keepsake, around her neck—but he was a major flirt and confessed to at least one affair in addition to Angelica. The sisters remained devoted throughout. The town of Angelica located in western New York, was named by Philip Church after his mother.

Someone gave us this recipe and said they were served at the Schuylers' holiday parties in the 1700s. We don't know if that's true, but they are really good anyway.

Schuyler House Spice Cookies

Cream:
¾ cup of butter
1 cup of sugar

Add:
1 egg
¼ cup of molasses
Then add: (all together now)
2 cups of flour
2 teaspoons of baking soda
¼ teaspoon of salt
1 tablespoon of cinnamon

1 tablespoon of cloves
1 tablespoon of coriander
1 tablespoon of ginger
A small dash of pepper

Roll dough into small balls and then roll each ball around on a plate of sugar to coat. Bake at 350 degrees for 10 minutes. Makes between 3 and 4 dozen cookies.

Two Super Stephens

Stephen Myers

Not many people in Albany are aware of the part the city played in the Underground Railroad (UR) and even fewer are familiar with Stephen Myers, a freed slave, who was one of the main activists in this area.

Stephen Myers was born a slave in Rensselaer County in 1800. He was freed at 18 and worked a number of jobs in the upstate region. He was an outspoken proponent of the antislavery movement and with his wife, started publishing a paper called the *Northern Star and Freeman's Advocate* in 1842. He held meetings at his house and aided great numbers of fleeing slaves by giving them a safe house and assistance in getting to Canada. Conductors on the UR in this area were very open with their reporting of how many people they helped; Stephen Myers helped 287 slaves in a 10-month period. What's amazing is that his house is still standing at 194 Livingston Street (formerly Lumber Street). This historic site was saved by Mary Liz and Paul Stewart, who have invested a number of years researching and teaching about the history of the UR in Albany. They give walking tours on the subject (Underground History Railroad Project, 432-4432) during the warm months.

Myers worked for the cause between 1830 and the 1850s. He died on February 13, 1870 in Albany. Look for his house to open as a living museum in the future. To help, you can contact the Stewarts at the Underground Railroad History Project.

Stephen Van Rensselaer III

This Stephen, not number II or IV, definitely deserves a special hooray in the history of this area. Not because he was a patroon, which was a bad thing, but because he was the last patroon, and was actually called "The Good Patroon."

Stephen III was born in New York City in 1764, but grew up here in the Van Rensselaer Manor House. His mother was a Livingston, his uncle was Abraham Ten Broeck, and when his father died, his mother married Domine Westerlo. You probably recognize these names. Stephen graduated from Harvard at age18 (after his education at Princeton was interrupted by those pesky British) and a year later, on June 6, 1783, when he was just 19, he eloped with Margarita, one of the Schuyler daughters. He and Margarita had three children. After her death in 1801, he married the daughter of New Jersey's governor, Cornelia Patterson, with whom he had another 10 children.

When Stephen was 21 years old he took control of the family estate or patroonship. In the early days of Albany's development, the Dutch wanted as many warm bodies here as possible to protect their trade interests against any other group of immigrants. They initiated a patroon system, which was basically a feudal system, where they would give away large tracts of land to a patroon for bringing over 50 settlers. Killian Van Rensselaer knew a good thing when he saw it and took full advantage of this deal. Although he never personally set foot here, his heirs were plentiful and everywhere. When the English took over, they respected this arrangement and let the patroons live on. They changed the terminology slightly and the patroons became landlords, charging their tenants rent and taxes on the land they worked. After the American Revolution, you can imagine how the hard-working tenants began to feel about this system.

Stephen III, having inherited a huge amount of land and seeing no easy way to take care of it, concocted a scheme to entice farmers to settle on his land. He offered 120 acres, free for 7 years to anyone who would clear and maintain the land. They would receive a lease at the end of the 7 years, but could not see that lease until the 7 years was up. After the "free" period was over, the farmers were shocked to find that they weren't given title to the land but instead were expected to pay rent, taxes, and supply free labor to the patroon (Stephen III) without having any rights to the water, timber, or anything else that might be on their land. This marked the beginning of the end.

Stephen III knew it would be hard to collect the rent so in large part, he let it slide, making him "The Good Patroon." This however, backfired on his son, Stephen IV who, upon his father's death in 1839, had to pay all of his father's debts ($400,000) and was directed to use back rents, to do so. Sure, like that was going to work.

The Antirent Wars began in upstate New York almost immediately and lasted until 1846. This was a hard-fought battle between the farmers and law enforcement. The militia was called in to quell the insurrection when a deputy sheriff was killed in 1845. The resistance turned to politics and elected John Young as governor who pushed the state to amend its constitution and outlawed long-term leases.

About 15 years before his death, Stephen III decided it was time for a learning institute "for the purpose of instructing persons, who may choose to apply themselves, in the application of science to the common purposes of life." And so, in 1824 the Rensselaer School got its start.

It would become the Rensselaer Institute 10 years later (RPI today), and in 1835, eight women graduated, completing a special mathematics course. Stephen III served his state out of a sense of duty, working in the Assembly, Senate, and as lieutenant governor of New York, pushing for unpopular reforms like extended suffrage. He served on the Canal Commission from 1816 to 1839. RPI actually had a summer session in 1830 on the "Rensselaer School Flotilla" on the Erie Canal. He died in 1839 and was buried in the family plot but was moved to Albany Rural Cemetery when the manor was moved to Williams College (to be used as a frat house, but demolished in 1973) and everybody had to move—dead or alive.

Three Thrilling Henrys

Henry Hudson

September 19, 2009 marked the 400th anniversary of Henry Hudson's arrival in the Albany area. Even though settlers did not start arriving to actually build the forts, and eventually the city, until years later (Fort Orange was built in 1624), we will go along with the 1609 date as one of our anniversaries. It has a nice ring to it. As is often the case, we didn't care much about who Hudson was until after he became famous for his journey in which he sailed up the Hudson River on the Half Moon. He died 2 years later, and so, we don't know a whole lot about him. There isn't even an actual likeness of him, just drawings made from recollections well after his death.

Most scholars go along with 1570 as his year of birth and possibly September 12 being his actual birthday. It is generally assumed that he got in a lot of sailing experience as a young man, but the only recorded trips are the biggies in which he was searching for the Northeast or

Northwest passages to get to the silks and spices of Asia for various trading companies. His grandfather had a controlling share in the Muscovy Company, so his first two important trips on his quest to sail over the north pole, were for his grandfather's company (in 1607 and 1608). The trip that put Albany on the map was the voyage of 1609.

Henry was a man on a mission at this point and was bent on finding that Northwest passage, which he believed he would locate in America, following the Grand River (named by Verrazano in 1524 while working for the French, who were actually the first Europeans to be trading here, in the 1500s) over the top of the world. This river would become the Hudson. In January 1609 he signed a contract with the Dutch East India Company, which guaranteed him payment of 800 guilders to make the trip, and his wife 200 guilders if he didn't make it back alive. In turn, he promised to deliver to the company all of the information he would gather, including all of his logs with nothing held back. Not widely known, is that two ships—the Half Moon and the Good Hope—were sent out together on that March 25, heading north first and then west. The crew of the Good Hope mutinied when it was decided to head across the Atlantic after the voyage north had failed.

What is interesting here, is that Hudson's logs for 1607, 1608, and 1610–1611 have all been reprinted, but the one that would mean the most to Albany, was sold at auction in 1821 with other papers from the Dutch East India Company and basically vanished. Our information about that trip is mostly taken from the journal of Robert Juet. Hudson and Juet disliked each other, but Hudson hired him three times, twice as mate. Although an expert sailor, some referred to Juet as Hudson's evil genius. On the Half Moon voyage, a Dutch sailor was actually the first mate.

Sadly for Hudson, the big river provided no outlet to Asia. In fact, shallow water forced him to stop his trip at Albany. He anchored here for 4 days trading with the locals, before heading back to Europe. He thought he would stop off in Dartmouth on his way back to Amsterdam (he arrived in Dartmouth on November 7, 1609). Hudson was promptly arrested for treason (sailing under another country's flag) and the Half Moon and its Dutch crew sailed back to Amsterdam with Hudson's logs and booty. Once released from his "arrest," and never being one who gave up, Hudson tried one last time to find the elusive passage, this time sailing for the British East India Company, with the ship Discovery. Although arriving in Hudson Bay in August, Hudson spent too many months mapping the shores and ended up stuck in the ice for the winter. The crew was pretty unhappy at this point, including first mate Juet. When the ice finally melted the following June, Juet instigated a mutiny and dumped Hudson, his son John, and eight of his loyal crew into a small boat and left them to die in the open waters of Hudson Bay. Presumably they did. However, a 150-pound rock was found by a road crew up near Hudson Bay more than 40 years ago which had carved into it "HH 1612 CAPTIVE." So who really knows for sure?

Hudson left behind a wife and two sons. His wife went on to become a wealthy woman, working for the English East India Company.

Here is another secret family recipe. This one is from our Hungarian gypsy aunt who was one of the best bakers we knew.

Half Moon Cookies

Cream:
2 sticks of butter
¾ cup of sugar
2 teaspoons of vanilla
1 tablespoon of water

Add:
½ teaspoon of salt
2 cups of flour
6 oz. of finely chopped pecans

When this is all blended, shape into small crescents (or half moons) and place on an ungreased cookie sheet.

Bake at 350 degrees for about 20 minutes until slightly golden.

When cool enough to handle, put them in a bag with ¼ cup confectioner's sugar and shake gently until coated. Refrigerate them so this sticks and then coat them again, this time with ½ cup confectioner's sugar.

You good cooks out there will notice there is no leavening in these cookies, and yes that is correct.

Henry Hobson Richardson

We really like Henry Hobson Richardson. He is known as the first American architect and Albany is home to two of his glorious buildings. He was the last architect working on the capitol and then he designed City Hall across the street. In Troy, the Gardner Earl Chapel was built in the Richardsonian Romanesque style 2 years after Richardson's death.

Richardson was born September 29, 1838 in Louisiana. He was one of four children. He was raised in New Orleans and was called "Fez" by his family and friends. At age 18 he went off to Harvard and from there, to the Ecole des Beaux Arts in France. He was only the second American to be accepted to study there. Upon returning home, he married Julia, the sister of a Harvard classmate, and had six children. He began his career immediately with a commission to build the Church of the Unity in Massachusetts in 1866.

Richardson wasn't interested in designing buildings in the popular Victorian Gothic styles, but took his inspiration from the medieval period. He was so into the 11th century that he often roamed around in monk's robes. You can Google his image and see a number of photographs of him wearing a monk's outfit. His style reflected him. It was massive and dramatic. Richardson was well over 6-feet-tall and weighed more than 300 pounds. He died on April 27, 1886 at age 48. Although his design career was cut short, of 10 buildings voted in 1885 as the most successful examples of architectural design in the country, 5 were designed by Richardson and 2 of those are Albany's very own City Hall and State Capitol. Trinity Church in Boston was voted No. 1, but that's a pretty nice building, too.

Richardson considered the Marshall Field Wholesale Store he designed in Chicago, one of his last, to be one of his most significant works. It was demolished in 1930 to put up a parking lot.

Joseph Henry (OK we cheated a bit here)

Next time you're downtown, walk through the conifer garden near the old Albany Academy. In front, there is a statue of Joseph Henry, one of America's greatest scientists. A physics genius!!!! The stone marker is engraved with the story of his electromagnetic bell ringing in Albany. It is very hard to read, as the U's are all V's, and over time it's gotten a bit fuzzy. However, this guy really did something great, and right here.

Joseph Henry was born in Albany on December 17, 1797. His parents were very poor and after his father died, he lived with his grandmother in Galway. The elementary school he attended is named for him. He had a number of jobs including sales clerk, watchmaker, and silversmith. He also had thoughts of becoming an actor. When he was 16, he read a book on scientific lectures and his life's path totally changed. He received free tuition to attend the Albany Academy in 1819 when he was 22. Still broke, he earned extra money by teaching and tutoring privately. His teachers realized that he was smarter than they were, and he was appointed a professor of mathematics and the natural sciences at Albany Academy in 1826. He started dabbling in electricity in his spare time and came up with what he called his intensity magnet (an electromagnet based on one by Sturgeon). He built the most powerful one of his time: a magnet that could hold 1,000 pounds and with a touch of a button, electrode actually, he could drop it. He amazed his students by running a mile's worth of wire throughout Albany Academy and connecting his electromagnet at one end so that it rang a bell at the other end. Basically, a long-distance telegraph. Samuel Morse is credited with the invention of the telegraph, but it was Henry's design, made a little better AND 10 years later.

Henry became a professor at Princeton in 1832. In 1846, The U.S. government was ready to spend the money bequeathed to them by James Smithson of London for the Smithsonian Institute, to promote science and spread knowledge, and wanted Henry to head it up. He was asked to be its first secretary. Henry really did not want to leave Princeton where he could continue with his research in electricity but he went anyway. At the Smithsonian, he was sought after for his advice and help on new technologies of the day. In 1875, Alexander Graham Bell came to talk about his little idea—called the telephone. Bell perfected this idea and showed it off to Henry at the Smithsonian in 1877.

Joseph Henry died on May 13, 1878. In science, a unit of induction is called a henry. Definitely, one Albany boy who made good!

Four Famous Phils of Albany

Philip Livingston

Philip Livingston was born in Albany on January 15, 1716 to one of Albany's prominent (or shall we say rich and powerful) families. His family home was at the corner of State and North Pearl streets. A Starbucks sits in its place now. (There is a plaque on the outside wall to tell you this.) On this site in the 1730s, young Philip planted an elm tree that stood on this corner until it was taken down on June 15, 1877. The tree became a landmark and the corner was known as Elm Tree Corner for years after the tree was gone. It also was known as Hanging Elm Tree Corner and many were hung until dead from the tree's limbs, including two young slaves (12- and 14-year-old girls) accused of setting the fire of 1793 that destroyed more than 60 buildings on Broadway, including the Ten Broecks' mansion.

Livingston graduated from Yale in 1737 and settled in New York. He married one of the Ten Broecks, with whom he had several children. He became more and more involved in the politics of the day and we are talking American Revolution politics of the day. He had been a delegate to the Albany Convention in 1754 but by the time the 1770s rolled around he became a very vocal supporter of the idea of America's separation from Britain. He was a delegate to the Continental Congress in 1775 and was one of the signers of the Declaration of Independence in 1776. He was elected to the New York State Senate in 1777, but died suddenly the next year. He is buried in York, Pennsylvania.

Philip Schuyler

Philip Schuyler was born on November 11, 1733, to one of the wealthiest families in Albany. Schuylerville, Schuyler Flats, Schuyler Bakery, you know the name. He married Catherine Van Rensselaer in September 1755, just 5 months before the birth of their first daughter, Angelica. Human gestation was apparently much shorter in colonial times. They were a devoted couple producing, 11 children, 8 of whom survived.

During the French and Indian War (1755–1760) he commanded a company in New York. After the war he busied himself running a very large estate left to him by his father. As the colonies were becoming more and more disgruntled with British rule, much like Livingston, Schuyler took up the cause. He was one of four major generals appointed under Washington. Schuyler's job was to plan and implement an attack against Canada. Because of his poor health, he turned over this plan to Gen. Richard Montgomery. However, Schuyler had been too slow executing his plans for this attack and it failed. In 1777, British Gen. John Burgoyne managed to win the northern stronghold of Fort Ticonderoga due to perceived incompetence on Schuyler's part. Schuyler demanded a court martial to clear his name. He was acquitted of any wrongdoing, but resigned his post soon thereafter. He then became involved in local politics and served as a New York State senator for 13 years. He served as a U.S. senator for one term before losing his seat to Aaron Burr. Yes, the Aaron Burr that killed Schuyler's son-in-law Alexander Hamilton. Burr won the seat in the senate due to the efforts of the Livingston and Clinton families. And yes again, that Livingston family. Schuyler won the seat back in 1797 with the help of Hamilton. The grudge match between Burr and Hamilton continued until Burr killed Hamilton in a duel in 1804. Schuyler died in November 1804, a few months after the death of his beloved wife Catherine and his beloved son-in-law Hamilton. In 1925, a statue of Philip Schuyler by J. Massey Rhind was erected in front of Albany's City Hall.

Philip Hooker

You may not be familiar with the name, but Philip Hooker was one of Albany's foremost architects in the late 1700s. Hooker was born October 28, 1766 in Rutland, Massachusetts. His parents, Samuel and Rachel, were married a few months earlier in the previous July. (Again, the gestation period was much shorter back then.) Samuel was a carpenter and a builder and it was from his father that Philip learned the trade. Philip and his family moved to Albany when he was 6 years old and he stayed here until his death in 1836.

Hooker was very involved in local government and served as Albany's assessor seven times and as city superintendent and city surveyor. He began designing and building a lot of Albany's buildings at this time, not so much because he was a brilliant architect but because he was known and trusted.

By 1833, after his heyday as an architect, if you looked around Albany, five churches, all three banks in town, both schools including Albany Academy, City Hall, the state capital, 3 downtown markets, the

Proctor Leland and Pearl Street theaters and numerous private homes, all were designed by Hooker. There was literally, a Hooker on every corner in Albany. Hooker's style was borrowed from old or cast-off styles from Europe. What was old to Europe became fashionable to Albany. When other New Englanders arrived in Albany after the Revolution, Albany had a very medieval feel to it. They insulted Albany by calling it "more Dutch than decent." Hooker's buildings gave Albany a more stately appearance.

Hooker was married twice but had no children. He is buried with his first wife in the Albany Rural Cemetery. Almost every Hooker building has been demolished, destroyed by fire, or remodeled beyond recognition but there are still a few left in town including First Church on North Pearl, the original Albany Academy, which is now the Albany Board of Education building, and a once private home, which is now Angel's Bed and Breakfast at 96 Madison Avenue. In Troy, the Hart-Cluett mansion also is one of Hooker's designs.

Philip Sheridan

Did you ever wonder who that guy was on the horse in front of the state capitol? A very impressive looking man on a very impressive looking horse. The man was Gen. Philip Sheridan and the horse was named Rienzi. The horse was a 16-hand Morgan (that's a pretty tall horse) and jet black. Sheridan on the other hand was 5'5 in his boots, nicknamed "Little Phil," and said to have had to shimmy up his saber to get up into his saddle. Lincoln said he had such long arms that if his ankles itched he could scratch them without stooping. Hooray for artistic license!

Sheridan was born on March 6, 1831, some say in Albany, others Ohio and some say on the boat coming over from Ireland. At 17, Sheridan decided it was Albany. He did grow up in Ohio and was eventually admitted to West Point in New York where it took him 5 years to graduate. Apparently, he was held back for fighting with another cadet. Although not an impressive student, he became an outstanding commander, rapidly rising to major general during the Civil War. On October 19, 1864, at the crucial battle of Cedar Creek in Virginia's Shenandoah Valley, Sheridan riding on top of the magnificent Rienzi, rallied his demoralized and panicked troops to victory. "Sheridan's Ride" by Tom Read was a poem written about this famous ride and was published everywhere in the north to promote the Union war effort.

Rienzi saw 19 battles and was wounded several times. When Rienzi died at a pretty good age at his master's home, Sheridan had him stuffed and put on display in the first U.S. Army Museum in Manhattan, which was destroyed by fire in 1922. Rienzi, however, was saved and escorted to the Smithsonian Museum, where you can see him today encased in glass in the Hall of Armed Forces History.

Sheridan is universally hated by Virginians because he was responsible for burning Virginia down to ensure the Union win in the Shenandoah Valley. In 1865, he pursued Gen. Robert E. Lee and was instrumental in Lee's forced surrender at Appomattox. After the Civil War, Sheridan served in the Department of the Missouri where his job was to crush the Plains Indians. He was accused of genocide and racism and given credit for the wonderful quote "the only good Indians I ever saw were dead." He steadfastly denied saying this.

In 1875, he married Irene Rucker with whom he had four children. He died after a series of heart attacks on August 5, 1888. After his death, his wife never remarried and said she would rather be the widow of Phil Sheridan than the wife of any living man. The statue of Sheridan and Rienzi was unveiled in front of the State Capitol Building in October 1916. In a letter to Gov. Charles S. Whitman a year earlier, Mrs. Sheridan protested that the planned memorial statue "did not bear any resemblance to her husband," however, she was overruled by committee.

Get Off the Couch!!!!

There really is a lot to do in and nearby the capital region. This is a list of things we have found that you might enjoy.

Recreations for Your Body

Snowshoeing

Five Rivers Environmental Center: 56 Game Farm Road, Delmar, 475-0291. Snowshoes can be rented for $3 a pair for use on the grounds of the environmental center. The center features more than 10 miles of hiking trails. It is open Monday through Saturday, 9 a.m. to 4:30 p.m. and Sundays, 1 to 4:30 p.m. Cross-country skiing is available, as well.

Albany Pine Bush Preserve: New Karner Road, Albany, 456-0655. Around 18 miles of marked trails are waiting for you to explore or you can take a guided snowshoe walk (snow shoes provided). Call for reservations.

Downhill Skiing

You can find a number of resorts nearby online including Bousquet, Hunter, Jiminy Peak, Gore, and Windham but locally:

Maple Ski Ridge: 2725 Mariaville Road, Schenectady, 381-4700. This is a small, family-owned ski slope just off exit 25A, less than 5 miles from downtown Schenectady. All levels of skiing and snowboarding, as well as lessons are available. You will enjoy nice views of the hills from the warming/snack bar lodge.

Cross-Country Skiing

Available for free or for a small fee at most of the public golf courses including:

Schenectady Municipal Golf Course: 400 Oregon Avenue, Schenectady 382-5155.

Town of Colonie Golf Course: 418 Consaul Road, Schenectady, 374-4181.

Free at the state and local parks including:

The Crossings: 580 Albany-Shaker Road, Colonie, 438-5587.

Dyken Pond Environmental Center: 475 Dyken Pond Road, Cropseyville, 658-2055.

Grafton Lakes State Park: 61 North Long Pond Road, off Route 2 (12 miles east of Troy), Grafton, 279-1155.

John Boyd Thacher State Park: Route 157 (15 miles southwest of Albany or 1 Hailes Cave Road if you are using your GPS), Voorheesville, 872-1237.

Normanskill Farm Park: Mill Road, Albany. For information, call the city at 434-2489.

Peebles Island State Park: 10 Delaware Avenue, Cohoes, 237-8643.

Cross-country skiing also is allowed on most bike trails.

For a fee:

Oak Hill Farms Cross Country Ski Center: 1206 Oak Hill Road, Esperance, 875-6700. There are more than 30 km of trails on the 500-acre farm, with trails for beginners and experts.

Ice Skating

If you have your own skates, see if they have ice on the Empire State Plaza for public skating. Or:

Hudson Valley Community College: 629-4850. Public skating is available on Saturday and Sunday.

Town of Colonie: The Crossings pond or at Town Hall's pond, 785-4301.

Knick Arena: 103rd Street and Eighth Avenue, Lansingburg, 235-7761. Public skating also is offered.

Places to Walk

Walking is free and is the best way to get in shape with very little effort. But where to walk? Besides Washington Park, which is the obvious place if you live in downtown Albany, there are a number of other locations that you can get to easily.

Corning Preserve: 434-2032. The preserve has miles of walkways along the Hudson River.

Five Rivers: 56 Game Farm Road, Delmar (mentioned above). There are 10 miles of trails through the nature preserve.

The Albany Rural Cemetery: 48 Cemetery Avenue, Menands, 463-7017.

Vale Cemetery: 907 State Street, Schenectady, 346-0423.

Oakwood Cemetery: 186 Oakwood Ave: 4 Central Avenue, Albany, 463-5145.

The Schuyler Flats Cultural Park: Route 32, Menands. This is a 43-acre park with soccer and softball fields and surrounded by a walking trail. There is easy access to the bike trail along the Hudson.

Lions Park: River Road, Niskayuna. This is a nice little park with access to a beautiful stretch of hike and bike trail along the Mohawk River. Walking west from the park, you will reach Lock 7 of the Erie Canal, which is worth the detour. You can park at either Lions Park or at Lock 7, which is just a little further down on River Road from the park.

The Crossings: 580 Albany-Shaker Road, Colonie. Located on 130 acres, The Crossings has 6.5 miles of paved trails for walking, biking, skating, or taking the dog out for a run.

Rensselaer Tech Park: Located in East Greenbush this is not actually a park, but it is also active with walkers who want to steer clear of traffic.

Hiking

These places offer a walk with a bit more challenge.

Albany Pine Bush Preserve: 195 New Karner Road, Albany, 456-0655. The preserve, located in a historical pine barren, has more than 3,000 acres with miles of well-marked trails The only complaint we have with this park is the amount of noise, which just can't get be avoided. The noise from the highway and rifle range interrupts what could be a wonderful walk.

Dyken Pond: Follow the signs off Route 7 east of Troy. This place is way off the beaten path but worth a look. If you take the paths off to the wooded farm trail you'll get a much longer hike in. First, there are miles of trails. But second, they are horribly marked so that you could get lost for days on them. We like hiking in the winter and thankfully there are always dog tracks that lead us back to the parking lot.

Grafton Lake: Again follow Route 7, this time way east of Troy. Although the hike around Long Lake is supposed to be only a couple of miles, the terrain makes it feel like many more. This is a state park that, in addition to having well-marked, beautiful hiking trails, also offers swimming and boating.

Normanskill Farm: Mill Road, left off Delaware right before the bridge to Delmar. This park/historic site offers miles of hiking along the Normanskill River and rolling hay fields. The farm dates back to the 1600s and there are some cool remnants of the old ice house next to the river. There is a dog park here for off-lead activities but you can take your dog on the trails while leashed. Not a big parking area, but one of the nicest parks around for walking in, or just sitting by the water. There is even an actual yellow brick road here that is more than 200 years old.

Get Your Dog Off the Couch Too!

Dog Parks

If you live in one of the suburbs surrounding Albany, you probably have your own, resident-only dog park. Delmar, Niskayuna, and Guilderland have very nice off-leash dog parks for use by residents, but they have a yearly fee and residence requirements to use. Most of the public parks allow any leashed dogs, if you pick up after them.

Albany has four, very nice off-leash parks, open dawn to dusk, year-round. The rules are simple. You have to stay with your dog, clean up after your dog, and if your dog is not good with the other dogs, he has to go home.

Department of General Services Off-Lead Area: Erie Boulevard, off Erie Street, north of Huck Finn's Warehouse. This is a nice sized park with plenty of run room, a gazebo and picnic table for you, and hoses and a drinking fountain for water. If you have tiny dogs, walk the perimeter as there are a couple of spots that a little dog could squirm through.

Normanskill Farm Dog Park: Off Delaware Avenue, heading toward Delmar take Mill Road on the left, just before the bridge that goes over the Normanskill. The park is not very well marked so really watch for Mill Road. Take this road down to the parking area. You have to park in the first parking lot and then walk back to the community gardens and dog park. This is another good-sized park, but no gazebo for you. The (city-owned) farm has miles of trails that your leashed dog is more than welcome to hike with you.

Hartman Road Dog Park: Off New Scotland Road on Hartman Road. The park is almost immediately on your left, next to the community gardens. This is a smaller space, but has a few trees and a couple of places for you to sit. If you blink, you will miss the turn off for this park, so stay alert!

Westland Hills Dog Park: This is just off Colvin Avenue, behind the Armory car dealership. Look for the sign for the Frank Waterson Park/ Westland Hills Park and you are there. This is a pretty small park. There are no tables, however, it is surrounded by trees, so it looks pretty nice.

Bowling

Some of the local lanes are:

Olympic Lanes: 92 Bridge Road, off Broadway, Menands, 465-3505. Located very close to Albany, this bowling center has 50 lanes.

Playdium Bowling Center: 363 Ontario Street, Albany, 438-0300. Yes there really is a nice bowling alley near downtown. The hours change seasonally, so call before you head out.

Spare Time Bowling Center: 375 Troy-Schenectady Road, Latham, 785-6694. If you are out and about and find yourself in Latham, this is a nice alley to stop by.

Sunset Lanes: 1160 Central Avenue, Albany, 438-6404. This clean bowling alley is located in a pretty building and has great pricing. The hours change seasonally, so check the Web site, www.bowlsunset.com, to be sure.

Uncle Sam Lanes: 600 Fulton Street, Troy, 271-7800. This is a neighborhood bowling alley with discount games on Tuesday nights.

Rock Wall Climbing

A.I.R.: 4C Vatrano Road, Albany, 459-7625. A.I.R features indoor rock climbing and spelunking.

Indoor Baseball

All-Stars Academy: 198 Troy-Schenectady Road (Route 2), Latham, 220-9140.

Roller Skating

Guptill's Arena: 1085 New Loudon Road (Route 9), Cohoes, 785-0660. This is roller skating at its best, with a beautiful, huge floor. There is nothing else like this around. Bring your own skates or rent here.

Dance

The Arts Center of the Capital Region: 265 River Street, Troy, 273-0552. The Arts Center offers classes in belly dancing.

EBA: 351 Hudson Avenue (corner of Lark and Hudson), 465-9916. EBA has a full lineup of all types of dance classes that you can take. The cost of a semester is amazingly cheap and it's a great workout besides.

Exercise Classes

The Movement Lab: 225 River Street, Troy, 833-0402. The Movement Lab offers Pilates classes.

The Center for Nia–Yoga: 4 Central Avenue, Albany, 463-5145. The center offers classes in Nia exercise/dance.

YMCA: Area YMCAs are located in Albany (North Washington Avenue and Empire Plaza), Bethlehem, Clifton Park, Glenville, Greenbush, and Troy (http://www.cdymca.org/). All YMCAs offer exercise programs.

There are a number of gyms you can join in the area including Gold's Gym (Latham).

Skateboarding

Shelter Skate Park: 35 Commerce Avenue, 438-2228 (near Everett Road), Albany. Looking for a place to legally do a half-pipe on your skateboard? The Shelter is an indoor skate park with some modest ramps for you to practice on. The cost is $14 per session or $10 if you are a member.

Mini-Golf and Fun Parks

A Knight's Tale Mini-Golf: Route 9, Latham, 786-8725. This is a castle-themed course.

Control Tower: 1050 Troy-Schenectady Road, Latham, 782-9242.

Funplex Funpark: 589 Columbia Turnpike, East Greenbush, 477-2651.

Hoffman's Playland: 608 Loudon Road (Route 9), Latham, 785-3842. This is still a fun little place to take the kids. It's been a Latham landmark forever and is right next to the mini-golf course and ice cream.

Pirate's Hideout Inc.: 175 Guideboard Road, Halfmoon, 373-8438. There are no pirates here, but lots of water, and OK ice cream.

Apple Picking

Check our list of local orchards for fruit and berry picking in our shopping guide under FOOD.

Recreation for Your Mind and Soul

Museums

There are a ton of them, including:

The Albany Heritage Area Visitor's Center Museum: 25 Quackenbush Square, Albany, 434-0405. Nice museum with a good overview of the city's history. This museum offers a free orientation film.

Albany Institute of History and Art: 125 Washington Avenue, Albany, 463-4478. The entrance fee is $10 adults, seniors $8, $6 children ages 6 to 12. Entrance is free for Albany's First Friday. This museum offers a great glimpse into Albany's past with great changing exhibits.

N.Y. State Museum at Empire State Plaza: 264 Madison Avenue, Albany, 474-5877. This is always a fun experience, with new art exhibits.

Crailo State Historic Site: 9 ½ Riverside Avenue, Rensselaer, 463-8738. This is where "Yankee Doodle" was written.

Shaker Heritage Museum: 875 Watervliet-Shaker Road, Colonie (near the airport), 456-7890. This museum is the oldest Shaker settlement. It is situated on 770 acres with eight of the original buildings, a beautiful herb garden, orchard, Ann Lee Pond, and the Shaker cemetery. Saturday tours are offered and special events are held during the year.

Call the Mayor

If you have a good idea to share, the mayor does a live call in radio show on TALK 1300 (1300 AM) Fridays from 9 to 10 a.m. The number is 476-1300.

Volunteer

That's right. Do something for someone else today. Go to www.volunteermatch.org and find close to 150 things you can do including building for Habitat for Humanity; tutoring students in all subjects; helping with the Veggie Mobile, which distributes fresh produce; helping with all of Albany's special events; working at the animal shelters; and even measuring the snowpack in the Albany Pine Bush. You can volunteer at most of the local theater groups to make costumes, build sets, or just help out.

Go to the Movies

The Spectrum 8 Theaters: 290 Delaware Avenue, 449-8995. Downtown has the best indie theater around, offering a great choice of movies 365 days a year. And they have their own parking lots. Buy a 10-pack discount card and go often.

The Madison Theater: 1036 Madison Avenue in Pine Hills, 438-0040. This theater offers a selection of first-run blockbusters. Although not in great repair, this is a downtown theater that is easy for residents to get to. Street parking is pretty available most nights.

The Palace Theatre: 19 Clinton Avenue, 465-3334. Located downtown, this theater has a Monday night classic movie program that can be found on their Web site, www.palacealbany.com.

Open Mics

These are everywhere downtown and on different nights, so you can go out for a cheap night of really good music (and some not so good). No matter. They are all fun and for the price of a coffee you can have fun for a couple of hours. Here is a breakdown of some of them. Call for days and times.

The Daily Grind: 46 Third Street, Troy, 272-8658.

Elda's on Lark: 205 Lark Street, 449-3532.

Franklin's Tower: 414 Broadway, 431-1920.

Java Jazz Café: 318 Delaware Avenue, Delmar, 439-1727.

Moon and River Café: 115 S. Ferry Street, Schenectady, 382-1938.

The Muddy Cup: 1038 Madison Avenue, next to the Madison Theater, 458-6120.

The Muddy Cup: 432 State Street, Schenectady, 881-4515.

Tess' Lark Tavern: 453 Madison, 463-9779.

Friday Arts Nights

Held in downtown Troy, Albany, and Schenectady, you can enjoy art, music, and shopping. Albany: first Friday, Troy: last Friday, and Schenectady: third Friday of every month.

Go to the Theater

There is great local theater all over the capital district. Check *Metroland* or the *Times Union* Preview section for listings.

Albany Civic Theater: 235 Second Avenue, Albany, 462-1297.

Circle Theater Players: 2880 Route 43, Averill Park, 674-2007.

Classic Theater Guild: Performances at changing venues. To contact write: 217 Fourth Street, Troy, or call 441-2876.

Cohoes Music Hall: 58 Remsen Street, Cohoes, 237-5858.

Curtain Call Theater: 210 Old Loudon Road, Latham, 877-7529.

New York State Theater Institute (NYSTI): 37 First Street, Troy, 274-3200.

Park Playhouse: Located in Albany's Washington Park, 434-0776.

RPI Players: 110 Eighth Street, on the RPI campus, Troy, 276-6503.

Schenectady Civic Players: 12 South Church Street, Schenectady, 382-2081.

Schenectady Light Opera Company (SLOC): 826 State Street, Schenectady, 393-5732 or 1-877-350-7378.

Spotlight Players: Spotlight, like the Classic Theater Guild does not have its own performance space so venue can change. Great shows usually in East Greenbush at Columbia High School. Reach Spotlight at 210-9758

Steamer 10 Theater: 500 Western Avenue, 438-5503.

The Theater Barn: 654 Route 20, New Lebanon, 794-8989.

Art and Other Types of Classes

Albany Art Room: 457 Madison Avenue. Classes in drawing, printmaking, cartooning, and bookmaking for adults and children are offered at convenient times. There store on site where you can buy supplies so it is easy for you to get started on a more creative path. Visit albanyartroom.com for a full lineup of classes and times.

Arts Center of the Capital Region: 265 River Street, Troy, 273-0552. The Art Center offers classes in drawing, jewelry making, printmaking, stained glass, and a number of others, as well as yoga and belly dancing classes. Visit www.artscenteronline.org for more information.

Broken Mold Studio: 284 River Street, Troy, 273-6041. Pottery-making classes are offered for all ages. Go and get your hands dirty.

Knowledge Network: 1510 Central Avenue, Albany, 452-2675. Dozens of classes are offered in everything from painting to rose gardening, dancing to piloting an airplane. Check out their ever-changing selection at www.knowledgenetwork.org.

Planetariums and Stargazing

Henry Hudson Planetarium at the Albany Visitor's Center: 25 Quack-enbush Square, Albany, 434-0405. Planetarium shows are held on the third Saturday of each month at 11 a.m. and 1 p.m. The earlier show is more kid-friendly. Show prices are only $3.

Schenectady Planetarium: 15 Nott Terrace Heights, Schenectady, 382-7890. Shows are on Saturdays at 1, 2, and 3 p.m., and Tuesday through Friday at 2 p.m. Ticket prices are $10.25 for adults, $7.75 for children (kids under age 4 are free).

Hirsch Observatory: RPI campus, Troy, 423-3510. The Hirsch Observatory is open to the public on Saturday nights from February to mid-November, 8 to 10 p.m. From the observatory you can peer into the universe, right from Troy. There is parking on the street, as well as in the College Avenue parking lot. If it's cloudy, astronomy programs are held in Room 2C30 of the Science Center.

The Albany Area Amateur Astronomers, Inc. hosts its George Landis Arboretum Star Parties one weekend a month from March to November to share information and gaze upon the heavens. You are welcome to join them. For a schedule of dates, contact Susan French, 374-8460.

Take a Tour

Albany Aqua Ducks: 462-3825. The Aqua Duck is a fun way to tour the city and the river without having to change vehicles. Tours run about 75 minutes and reservations are strongly recommended. This tour is seasonal, but it's a pretty long season.

Capitol Tours: These tours of the State Capitol Building are free and are offered Monday through Saturday. Check the Web site for times.

Dutch Apple Cruises: Located at the Snow Dock at the Port of Albany, boarding at Madison Avenue and Broadway, 463-0220. A variety of cruises on the beautiful Hudson River are offered. Visit www.dutchapplecruises.com for descriptions and dates. These are seasonal cruises.

Walking Tours: Maps for these tours can be found at the Albany, Troy, and Schenectady visitor's centers. The historical societies also have scheduled walking tours during the year.

Art Galleries

Albany Center Gallery: 39 Columbia Street, Albany, 462-4775. A rich 30-year history now in new digs, the gallery offers a great place to see some of the outstanding creative work done by local artists.

Albany International Airport Gallery: Third floor at the airport, 242-2241. Yes the airport. This 2,500-square-foot space holds a couple of wonderfully curated exhibits every year. The gallery is open from 7 a.m. to 11 p.m. everyday and is FREE! It is well worth the visit and you can watch the planes take off next to the gallery.

The Arts Center of the Capital Region: 265 River Street, Troy, 273-0552. In the last few years, this center has really begun to shine. The shows are well curated and worth spending some real time looking at. The center offers dozens of classes and have performances in the Joseph L. Bruno Theater. Start enjoying it at Troy Night Out.

Clement Art Gallery: 201 Broadway, Troy, 272-6811. The gallery presents monthly exhibits, mostly from local artists. There is a large selection of framed and unframed art and framing is done on premises.

Fulton Street Gallery: 406 Fulton Street, Troy, 274-8464. This all volunteer-run gallery focuses on local artists.

Mandeville Gallery: 807 Union Street, Schenectady, 388-6000. Located on the second floor of the beautiful Nott Memorial on the Union College campus the gallery hosts new exhibits about three times a year.

Martinez Gallery: 3 Broadway, Troy, 274-9377. This is a contemporary gallery focusing on Latino and Latin American art. This gallery always impresses. Go in on the next Troy Night Out or any time and you will be amazed at the level of sophistication of each exhibit.

Esther Massry Gallery at the Massry Center for the Arts: 1002 Madison Avenue, Albany, 485-3902. This brand new facility on The College of Saint Rose campus features outstanding art and lectures from visual artists from around the world as well as the impressive work of students and faculty.

Opalka Gallery, The Sage Colleges: 140 New Scotland Avenue, Albany, 292-7742. A beautiful exhibit space that showcases faculty and student artwork.

NYS Museum Galleries: 264 Madison Avenue, Albany, 474-5877. The changing shows in the many galleries in the museum offer you a chance to see different art from around the country and from around the world. Some pretty amazing shows have passed through Albany in the last couple of years. It's a bargain to boot.

Photocenter, The Photography Center of the Capital District: 404 River Street, Troy, 273-0100. In addition to offering gallery space to its members, the Photocenter offers them studio space and equipment so they can pursue all aspects of photography. Basic membership begins at $35 per year. Visit the Web site at www.photocentertroy.org.

Upstate Artists Guild (UAG): 247 Lark Street, Albany, 426-3501. Exhibiting the art of more than 250 artists and administering Albany's First Fridays, UAG brings art to the masses. The guild hosts monthly gallery exhibitions as well as hosting different workshops. You can and should become a member and support the arts in Albany. Visit www.upstateartisisguild.org.

Worth an Outing, Galleries

The Sterling and Francine Clark Art Institute: 225 South Street, Williamstown, MA, (413)458-2303. Known for its collection of French Impressionist paintings—which are outstanding—the rest of the collection is pretty impressive (get it?) as well. Admission is FREE Nov. 1–May 31. The institute also features a library, and a café.

Tang Teaching Museum: 815 North Broadway, Saratoga, 580-8080. Located on the Skidmore campus, this museum focuses on contemporary art. Students and faculty from all disciplines in the college participate to develop exhibits throughout the year. The museum has 12 changing shows per year.

Music to Your Ears

You can find live music everywhere. Depending on what you prefer, local bars, small music venues, and some of the local college campuses offer a wide variety of music any night of the week. *Metroland* is a great source for finding out who's playing. (*Metroland* can be picked up for free all over the downtown area and the college campuses). The *Times Union* Thursday Preview section provides an overwhelming now-and-later rundown of who's performing where.

Here are the big and fairly big ones for famous acts:

The Times Union Center: Albany, timesunioncenter-albany.com.

Palace Theater: Albany www.palacealbany.com.

Washington Avenue Armory: Albany www.washingtonavenuearmory. com.

The Egg: Albany www.theegg.org.

EMPAC at RPI: EMPAC features experimental (and we mean experimental) music, theater, and dance. Visit the Web site at empac.rpi.edu.

Massry Center for the Arts at The College of St. Rose: This arts center also has a new performance space. Visit www.strose.edu/massry.

Proctor's in Schenectady: www.proctors.org.

The Troy Saving's Bank Music Hall: Troy, www.troymusichall.org.

Revolution Hall: Troy, www.revolutionhall.com.

Northern Lights: Clifton Park, www.northernlightslive.com.

Local colleges, including RPI and SUNY Albany, also sponsor bigger acts in their sports arenas. Check their calendars online.

Some of the smaller places, as well as clubs and bars around town, that feature music include:

Bread and Jam: 130 Remsen Street, Cohoes, 326-2275.

Franklin's Tower: 414 Broadway, Albany, 431-1920.

Jillian's: 59 N. Pearl Street, Albany, 432-1997.

Justin's: 301 Lark Street, Albany, 436-7008. The best live jazz in town is found here.

The Linda (WAMC): 339 Central Avenue, Albany, 465-5233.

McGeary's Pub: 4 Clinton Square, Albany, 63-1455 Check the pub's online calendar for bands.

The Moon and River Café: 115 S. Ferry Street, Schenectady, 382-1938.

Mothers at RPI: 15th Street, Troy, 276-6920. Visit mothers.union.rpi. edu for a schedule. Live music is featured every Friday and Saturday.

Positively 4th Street: 46 4th Street, Troy, 687-0064. This bar features live music, specifically, rock and roll.

Red Square: 388 Broadway, Albany, 465-0444. Featuring a live music venue and a dance floor, the Red Square is located across from the D&H building in the SUNY Plaza.

Savannah's: 1 South Pearl Street, Albany 426-9647. Offers live music.

Tess' Lark Tavern: 463 Madison Avenue, Albany, 453-9779. Open mic is held every Wednesday and comedy night is every third Saturday.

Valentines: 17 New Scotland Avenue, Albany, 432-6572. The Deadbeats perform here at 10 p.m. every Wednesday.

And Don't Forget!!!!!

Downtown Albany's Live at Five summertime concerts: These FREE concerts are held on Thursday nights at the Albany Riverfront Park at the Corning Preserve.

Lark St. BID's Monday Night in the Park: Outstanding free concerts are held in Washington Park in July and August.

Troy offers free concerts during the summer months at Riverfront and Powers parks. Check www.troyny.gov for event listings.

Especially for the Kids

Berkshire Bird Paradise Sanctuary and Botanical Gardens: 43 Red Pond Road, Petersburgh, 279-3801. Peter Durbacher has been running this sanctuary since 1975, caring for injured birds from across the country. Eagles, falcons, owls, and even unwanted chickens and wounded pigeons have made their home here. Those that can be rehabilitated are released, but those who cannot survive in the wild are given a loving home for the rest of their lives. All types of animals can be found here, even four-legged ones. There are even greenhouses where tropical plants are grown. The Durbachers run the sanctuary on donations and hard work alone. This is well worth the trip. The sanctuary is open from mid-May to October. Visit www.birdparadise.org for more information and directions.

New York State Museum: 264 Madison Avenue, across from the Empire State Plaza, Albany, 474-5877. This is a large museum containing New York history, artifacts, wildlife, and so on. The Cohoes mastodon is here, as is a working carousel from the early 1900s. Outstanding art exhibits can be viewed in the downstairs galleries. New exhibits are provided every year. The museum is open from 9:30 a.m. to 5 p.m. daily.

Schenectady Museum and Planetarium: 15 Nott Terrace Heights, Schenectady, 382-7890. This museum focuses on the scientific innovations that came out of this area. The planetarium has shows Tuesday through Saturdays.

Children's Museum of Science and Technology: 250 Jordan Road, Troy (in the Rensselaer Tech Park), 235-2120. Hands-on science exhibits, live exotic animals, and changing shows in the dome planetarium theater are the highlights here.

Albany Pine Bush Discovery Center: 195 New Karner Road, Albany, 456-0655. This center introduces you to the pine bush by showing just what makes this ecosystem so special. A few hands-on displays inside, but pick up the map and walk the trails to see it for yourself.

Five Rivers Environmental Education Center: 56 Game Farm Road, Delmar, 475-0291. Run by the New York State Department of Environmental Conservation, this 446-acre preserve offers 12 miles of trails winding through a diverse number of habitats. There are 16 ponds, fields, orchards, and woods supporting hundreds of species of birds, mammals, and creepy crawly things. The biggest bull frog we ever saw was in one of the ponds here. there even is an information center with exhibits and bathrooms.

Henry Hudson Planetarium at the Albany Visitor's Center: 25 Quackenbush Square, Albany, 434-0405. There are two shows on the third Saturday of each month (11 a.m. and 1 p.m.). The morning show is geared for kids aged 6 and under. Learn about the stars with interactive fun for only $3 per person.

Art classes are available for kids and adults at either the Albany Art Room (457 Madison Ave., Albany, 427-3910) and the Arts Center of the Capital Region (265 River Street, Troy, 273-0552).

Natural Science 101

New York state's mammal is the North American beaver, so the following is a brief introduction to that adorable rodent, which put Albany on the map. The beaver is the largest rodent in the United States and can get as large as 55 pounds. Some 14,000 years ago, a giant beaver that was about the size of a small black bear roamed North America. (The beaver is Canada's national animal so they have a replica of one of the giant ones in their natural history museum in Montreal.) Beavers mate for life and build their homes—dams—in streambeds and ponds. They use mostly soft wood trees like poplar, birch, and willow to do this. Dams can be more than 2,000-feet-long and 14-feet-high. Beavers are essential to preserving wetland habitats and often help to slow down water flow during flood seasons. The living quarters in the dams are upstairs and although beavers can hold their breath for 15 minutes, they are mammals and like nice dry places to live. The dam has an underwater entrance that keeps those pesky predators at bay. They eat water lily tubers, roots, and the inner bark of smaller trees, along with some berries and apples (in season, of course). They are "busy as a beaver" dawn through dusk and can work through the night to rebuild a downed dam. Beavers can live to 24 years in the wild, or until someone kills them for their fur, or up to 50 years in captivity. They are also considered an affable, playful animal.

The BIG List of Eating Out

This list includes coffee shops, diners, fancy restaurants, not so fancy restaurants, and pizza places.

Coffee Shops (Tea, Too)

There are at least 20 Starbucks in the Albany area if you really need that double caffeine kick start in the morning, however, the local coffee shops listed here offer something extra and we like them a lot.

Bread and Jam: 130 Remsen Street, Cohoes, 326-2275. This is a comfortable coffeehouse with an emphasis on live music. They have a musician-friendly performance area and have music 4 nights a week. Breakfast, goodies, and a light fare menu—you know sandwichy things. The Sunday jazz brunch is sometimes standing-room only so you might want to get there early. Bread and Jam is open 7 days a week with later hours on Fridays and Saturdays.

The Daily Grind: 46 Third Street, Troy, 272-8658. This Daily Grind has a really homey feel to it with couches and tables. The Daily Grind serves soups, sandwiches, and desserts, but it's the great open mic on Thursdays that keeps bringing us back. Oh and the coffee is good, too.

The Daily Grind: 204 Lark Street, Albany, 434-1482. This is the cozy downtown Albany coffee shop. It serves sandwiches, soups, desserts, and coffee like the Troy shop, only in a smaller setting.

Everybody's Café: 674 Columbia Turnpike, East Greenbush, 479-2233. This is a cute place located in an old house and features a great espresso menu, warming, delicious soups, and all-day breakfast. It is just a few doors down from The Sweater Venture, which is one of the great places to shop in the area.

Flavour Café and Lounge: 228 Fourth Street, Troy, 266-9253. This is an inviting establishment with more than 31 types of brewed coffees. They also feature light lunch and dinner menus.

The Good Leaf: 274 Lark Street, Albany, 434-0132. This is a quiet place to enjoy a cup of some really interesting teas and something sweet to go with it.

Java Jazz Café: 318 Delaware Avenue, Delmar, 439-1727. Located just outside of town, in Delmar, the café serves fresh-brewed, assorted gourmet coffees and teas, and breakfast and lunch made from local, organic ingredients. They feature a great assortment of homemade pastries. The café is open Monday through Friday, 7 a.m. to 7 p.m. and Saturday, 7 a.m. to 3 p.m.

Melville's Mug: 5 Clinton Square, across from the Palace Theater, 694-9991. This cozy coffee shop serves Green Mountain coffee, sandwiches, and soups and is open after the Monday night movies at the Palace.

Muddy Cup Coffee House: 1038 Madison Avenue, Albany, 458-6120. We are big fans of the coffee and pastries served here, but again, it is the open mic on Mondays that calls to us. Another Muddy Cup is located in Schenectady at 432 State Street (881-4515) and hosts its open mic night on Sundays at 7 p.m.

Professor Java's Coffee Sanctuary: 217 Wolf Road, Colonie, 435-0843. This is one of the most comfortable coffeehouses to hang out in. It serves great coffee, great food, and has a great atmosphere. It is open Monday through Thursday, from 7 a.m. to 11 p.m., Friday and Saturday, from 7 a.m. to midnight, and Sunday, 8 a.m. to 10 p.m.

Spill'n the Beans: 13 Third Street, Troy, 268-1028. This is another great place to hang out while enjoying your coffee. The chairs in the lounge area chairs are very comfortable and the fireplace makes it perfect. Offering a wide variety of interesting paninis and really good pastries, the coffeehouse is located across from the Uncle Sam Atrium in Troy, making it a convenient place to visit when you finish shopping at the winter farmer's market.

Restaurants

There are OK restaurants all over the capital district. Most of them serve variations on basic American family fare. In our listings, we focus on some exceptional restaurants with which we are familiar.

Fancy Fare

These are restaurants we usually reserve for visiting dignitaries, rich aunts, and anniversaries. They offer excellent food in an elegant setting.

Angelo's 677 Prime: 677 Broadway, Albany, 427-7463. Angelo's is a superior, but very expensive, steakhouse.

Café Capriccio: 49 Grand Street, Albany, 465-0439. *Metroland* named this the best restaurant for 2007 and no wonder. The gourmet Italian cuisine is phenomenal and the owner and staff make sure your dining experience is the best there is in Albany.

Daisy Baker's: 33 Second Street, Troy, 266-9200. Located across the street from the Troy Music Hall, this is an upscale establishment that serves good food.

Glen Sanders Mansion: 1 Glen Avenue, Scotia, 374-7262. A quality, contemporary American restaurant located in a colonial mansion. The service is outstanding.

Jack's Oyster House: 42 State Street, downtown Albany, 465-8854. An Albany landmark known as much for the politicians who eat there as the fine food, this restaurant features a contemporary American menu, but with some traditional fare.

The Hollywood Brown Derby: 22 Clinton Avenue, Albany, 463-1945. This is an elegant addition to Albany's downtown. This might be the place for you if you are looking for a special night out that has the feel of a different era.

LaSerre: 14 Green Street, Albany, 463-6056. Serving Continental cuisine, LaSerre is known for its veal Oscar and fresh pastas.

Marché: 74 State Street, Albany, 434-7410. Marché offers elegant French cuisine at prices you'd expect for such.

McGuires': 353 State Street at Lark, Albany, 463-2100. This restaurant features an excellent contemporary American menu in an informal setting.

Provence: Stuyvesant Plaza, Guilderland, 689-7777. Consistently top-rated by the *Times Union*, this restaurant serves French cuisine in a truly elegant setting.

The River Street Café: 429 River Street, Troy, 273-2740. Featuring contemporary American cuisine and an excellent wine list, the view of the Hudson in the evening completes the package.

Tosca Grille: 200 Broadway, Troy, 272-3013. This elegant and excellent restaurant is a wonderful contemporary American addition to Troy's downtown.

Yono's: 25 Chapel Street, Albany (located inside the Hampton Inn), 436-7747. Featuring an award-winning combination of Indonesian and continental dishes that are beautifully presented and delicious, Yono's is one of the best restaurants in the area.

Quality Specialty Restaurants

The restaurants on this list are mostly less-common, ethnic establishments and local favorites that consistently please the palate.

Albany Pump Station: 19 Quackenbush Square, Albany, 447-9000. Great food, great staff, and its own microbrewery, this restaurant is located in Albany's former pumping station, which was built in the 1870s and used until 1937. There is plenty of parking.

Al-Baraki II: 185 Lark Street, Albany, 445-0445. Al-Baraki serves up delicious homemade Lebanese food; however, you might be more comfortable taking the food to go as the seating is tight.

The Ale House: 680 River Street, Troy, 272-9740. This is a great place for traditional, soul-enriching pub food. It is open for lunch and dinner.

Ali Baba: 2243 15th Street, Troy, 273-1170. Serving Turkish fare, everything is delicious here. You must have the lavash bread fresh from the oven and try the cheese lover's pida for a change-of-pace pizza.

Antipasto's Vegetarian Bistro and Wine Bar: 1028 Route 146, Clifton Park, 383-1209. This restaurant features simply delicious, filling vegetarian cuisine in a small, very friendly place. This is a really nice surprise hidden inside a strip mall. They only accept cash, so come prepared.

Avenue A Restaurant: 544 Delaware Avenue, Albany, 434-2832. Outstanding, international, original cuisine is served by a super-friendly, attentive staff. The meals are HUGE so plan to share or take home. The macaroni and cheese with lobster is outrageous! This is a busy, noisy place you will love. It's a good idea to make a reservation if you are planning to dine after 7 p.m.

Beirut: 184 River Street, Troy, 270-9404. This Lebanese restaurant is located next to Bournebrook Antiques, and offers lots of tasty choices and wonderful falafel.

The Black Cat Ale House: 25 White Street, Cohoes 235-3199. Not what you would expect to find in Cohoes, this ale house has an extensive, delectable menu, all wonderfully prepared. Entrees range from $15 to $20.

Bombers Burrito Bar: 258 Lark Street, Albany, 463-9636. This Albany landmark serves burritos the size of babies. The bar is upstairs. A second establishment is now open at 447 State Street, Schenectady (374-3548).

Bros Tacos: 319 Ontario Street, Albany, 935-1098. This is a tiny take-out/eat-in Mexican restaurant located just off Madison with fresh home-made tortillas and delicious tacos and burritos. Two brothers really do own the place. Delivery is now available.

Brown's Brewing Co.: 417 River Street, 273-2337. Great pub fare, but as the name suggests, this also is a great (award-winning) brewery with a beautiful river view.

Bruegger's Bagels: 55 Congress Street, Troy, 274-4469. For a light breakfast or lunch, Bruegger's has the best bagels on Earth and this store is where it all started.

Café Madison: 1108 Madison Avenue, Albany, 935-1094. Breakfast is the most important meal of the day, so make it count by indulging at one of the best places around for breakfast. Lunch and dinner also are served. Plan on a little wait time, but rest assured, the food will not disappoint.

Café 217: 12½ Delaware Avenue, 462-0050. Open late night through lunchtime hours, the café features a fabulous breakfast menu. This is just what Albany needed for people looking for a non-diner place to get some great food after everyone else has gone to bed. It is notable for overnight hours, Wednesday through Saturday.

Caffe Italia: 662 Central Avenue, Albany, 459-8029. A cozy, casual place with exceptional food that makes you think you are in Italy. Crisp salads and delicious sauces highlight the fare here.

Capital Thai: 997 Central Avenue, Albany, 331-8854. This is the place for real Thai food with all the spicy flavors you crave.

Debbie's Kitchen: 456 Madison Avenue, Albany, 463-3829. This is your soup, sandwich, salad place extraordinaire. The desserts, especially the brownies, are fabulous.

El Loco Mexican Café: 465 Madison Avenue, Albany, 436-1855. El Loco's version of Tex-Mex. The food is good and reasonably priced.

El Mariachi: 144 Washington Avenue, 465-2568; 289 Hamilton Street, 432-7580 both in Albany. Good Mexican food is served in both friendly, comfortable places. At the Hamilton Street location you can enjoy the lively downstairs patio or go upstairs for a quiet dinner.

Famous Lunch: 111 Congress Street, Troy, 272-9481. This Troy landmark has been around since 1932, serving little hot dogs smothered in what is called "Zippy" sauce. You must experience these firsthand.

Franklin's Tower: 414 Broadway Albany, 431-1920. This Albany landmark is the place where the famous and powerful once hung out. Live music and food ranging from simple pub fare to full dinners. Take-out is offered as well.

The Ginger Man: 234 Western Avenue, Albany, 427-5963. Good food accompanies one of the best wine selections in the area.

Gus's Hot Dogs: 212 25th Street, Watervliet, 273-8743. Since the 1950s, Gus has been serving up these little hot dogs with a special meat sauce. This is a tiny, tiny place with a couple of picnic tables outside. The menu consists of hot dogs, hamburgers, and sausage sandwiches. You can get stuffed for under $5.

Hidden Café: Delaware Plaza at 180 Delaware Avenue, Delmar, 439-8800. This restaurant really is hidden, located off to the side of Friar Tuck's Book Store, but is really worth finding. Delicious, reallllly delicious Mediterranean offerings include falafel, kabobs, and unusual entrees.

Holmes & Watson: 450 Broadway, 273-8526. This is a good choice for lunch or dinner, featuring a large sandwich menu and more than 100 choices of beer and ale (25 beers on draft).

Ichiban: 338 Central Avenue, Albany, 432-0358. Don't like tofu? You will after trying Ichiban's orange tofu. Great Chinese and Japanese food that you can eat in or take out.

Iron Gate Café: 182 Washington Avenue, Albany, 445-3555. Delicious soups, sandwiches, and breakfasts—all a great deal.

Justin's: 301 Lark Street, Albany, 436-7008. Known for its live jazz (check www.justinsonlark.com for schedules), this is a fancier place with great food. Excellent pub fare is served at the friendly bar.

Karavalli: 9B Johnson Road, Latham, 785-7600. Not much from the outside, but the food is among the best Indian in the area. A nice buffet lunch is served.

Le Canard Enchaine: 25 Quackenbush Square, corner of Clinton and Broadway, Albany, 465-1111. Opened for business in 2008, this French restaurant offers up some great food in a warm, bistro setting. Prices are affordable and their prix-fixe lunch is one of the best deals around. Check www.le-canardenchaine.com for daily deals.

Legends Sports Lounge: 286 Lark Street, Albany, 275-4900. Offering great food and a great atmosphere, this is the best sports bar around.

Lombardo's Restaurant: 121 Madison Avenue, Albany, 462-9180. Albany used to have a very large Italian neighborhood where the Empire State Plaza currently is located. Although the neighborhood is gone now, some of the great restaurants stayed. Lombardo's is one of them. Its huge and tasty menu is a favorite of many Albanians.

Lo Porto's Ristorante Caffe (Lo Porto's): 85 Fourth Street, Troy, 273-8546. In our opinion, this is one of the best Italian restaurants anywhere. Everything is delicious and the portions are bountiful.

Mamoun's Falafel: 206 Washington Avenue, Albany, 434-3901. Mmm-mmm. Real falafel.

Manory's Restaurant: 99 Congress Street, Troy 272-2422. Manory's offers satisfying diner-type fare and a hearty breakfast is served all day.

Marmora Café: 203 River Street, 266-9300. Marmora serves Egyptian specialties. Stop by on Troy Night Out for a generous and really good gyro.

McGeary's Restaurant: 4 Clinton Square, Albany, 463-1455. A friendly Irish pub, McGeary's serves amazing appetizers.

Muza: 1300 15th Street at Congress Street, Troy, 271-6892. Polish/eastern European family fare is served in a small, friendly, family setting. Make sure to try the stuffed cabbage.

My Linh: 272 Delaware Avenue, Albany, 465-8899. My Linh serves delicious Vietnamese dishes in a really comfortable setting. Closed Mondays.

Plum Blossom: 685 Hoosick Road, Troy, 272-0036. Good Chinese food to go with incredible décor. Giant hand-carved wooden "somethings" tower over the central dining area.

Ristorante Paradiso: 198 Central Avenue, Albany, 462-5812. This Italian restaurant has been around a long time serving traditional favorites at good prices. The classic wall murals and stained glass really make you feel as though you have stepped into the past. This restaurant was used as a backdrop for Meryl Streep's song in the movie *Ironweed*, which was filmed in 1987.

Savannah's: 1 South Pearl Street, Albany, 426-9647. A small place that is really nice for lunch or dinner, Savannah's serves some really good appetizers, but has a small menu. Call for a schedule for live music. The bar is great.

Shalimar Restaurant: 35 Central Avenue, Albany, 434-0890; 407 Fulton Street, Troy, 273-8744; 15 Park Avenue, Clifton Park, 348-1494; and 180 Delaware Avenue, Delmar, 439-4200. These restaurants serve Indian fare, an inexpensive lunch buffet, and complete dinners. Every dish has its own distinctive flavor. Shalimar is Sanskrit for "temple of love" and you will love it here.

Sitar: 1929 Central Avenue, Albany, 456-6670. Sitar features classic and delicious Indian dining.

Sukhothai: 254 Lark Street, 463-0223; 62 Central Avenue, 433-7203. If you crave the flavorings of authentic Thai food, this is where to get it. There are numerous vegetarian choices and it is reasonably priced.

Sushi House: 6 New Scotland Avenue, Albany, 935-2270. Delicious fresh sushi is served, along with other Japanese fare, including tempura. The restaurant is closed Mondays.

Ultra Violet Café: 290 Delaware Avenue, Albany, 434-0333. Next to the Spectrum Theaters, this café is a great before or after the movie place. The food, especially the spinach pie, is yummy, and the service is really friendly.

Van's Vietnamese: 307 Central Avenue, Albany, 436-1868. Van's is an outstanding Vietnamese restaurant where everything is delicious, especially the spring rolls. The restaurant is closed Mondays.

Victory Café: 10 Sheridan Avenue, Albany, 463-9113. This is a friendly bar/restaurant with GREAT salads, good food, and a changing daily special. It is comfortable and inexpensive.

Pizza

There are pizza places all over town and we're sure you'll find one you like. Our short list in or near the downtown areas includes the following:

Big Apple Pizza: 108 14th Street, Troy, 271-4444. Located on the RPI campus, we love this pizza and you can pick up a large cheese pizza that is actually large, but with a small price.

Fountain Restaurant: 283 New Scotland Avenue, 482-9898.

J.G.'s Pizza: 195 Lark, Albany, 465-1922.

Jonathan's Pizza: 31 North Pearl Albany, 463-5100.

I Love NY: 850 Madison, Albany, 438-9400.

I Love Pizza: 125 Fourth Street, Troy, 274-0071.

Paesan's Pizza & Restaurant: 289 Ontario, Albany, 435-0312.

Pizza King: 124 Jay Street, Schenectady, 347-1234. This has been a favorite of ours for years. How did they luck out with that phone number?

SoHo Pizza: 269 Lark Street, Albany, 427-1111.

Worth a special trip:

DeFazio's Pizzeria: 266 Fourth Street in Troy's Little Italy, 271-1111. This is where you'll find wood-fired pizza with a crispy crust and tart sauce. The four-cheese pizza is sublime.

Diners

You can also find diners up and down Central and around town and they serve, well, diner food and are generally good. A couple of notables are:

Duncan's (Formerly Duncan's Dairy Bar): 890 Hoosick Road, Troy, 279-9985. We asked the waitress how long Duncan's has been here and she said since the dinosaurs roamed the earth. Some of the décor may date back that far, but it's hard to find such great, fresh, local food anywhere else. The wait staff is delightful and the chocolate shakes are the best in the area. You can get breakfast, lunch, or dinner everyday, anytime before 2 p.m., which is their closing time.

The Gateway Diner: 899 Central Avenue, Albany, 482-7557. Serving really good breakfasts, lunches, and dinners in their recently renovated diner, the Gateway has the friendliest wait staff.

Latham 76 Diner: 722 New Loudon Road, Latham, 785-3793. This diner has a couple of things going for it. First it's open 365 days a year! Second it is open 24 hours! The food and service are excellent as well, but this place has been a sanctuary for those who just need a quiet place to drink a cup of coffee when everyone else is sleeping.

The Miss Albany Diner: 893 Broadway, Albany, 465-9148. This is one of those tiny, historic diners where you'll have to duck to enter if you are over 6-feet-tall. Breakfasts are excellent and the lunch menu has some really intriguing, quite delicious fare. This is a breakfast and lunch place only, you might have to wait (worth it). Make sure you park on the street; if you park in the parking lot behind the diner your car will be towed.

Dining on the Hudson

There are three places that open just for the summer months. Here you can enjoy being on the river and eating at the same time.

Captain JP Cruise Line: 278 River Street, Troy, 270-1901. During the warmer months, the Captain runs dinner cruises up and down the Hudson. Call for the summer schedule or visit www.captainjp.homestead. com.

RiverFront Bar and Grill: 51 Erie Boulevard, in the Corning Preserve, Albany, 426-4738. Dine casually as you watch the boats go by. There is a full music lineup all summer.

The Rusty Anchor: 1 Selke Drive, Hudson Shores Park, Watervliet, 273-2920. Right across from Troy, this is comfortable barge dining with live music every weekend during the summer.

Special Note!! We haven't gotten to all of the area restaurants yet, but we consistently agree with Celina Bean who now does her reviews for the *Times Union* and usually has good information on newly opened places. Check out her page at www.celinabean.com.

Bar Districts

There are clusters of different bars and clubs throughout the area. The largest cluster is in downtown Albany. The big clubs can be found along Pearl Street and on Broadway in downtown. Smaller, more intimate bars can be found in the Lark Street area. College bars are found west of downtown along Madison Avenue, Western Avenue, and New Scotland

Road. In Troy, River Street north of the Green Island Bridge has a small row of very nice pubs. For major clubbing, Saratoga has a beautiful downtown with an extensive bar district.

The BIG Shopping List

This list includes food, clothing, thrift stores, pet supplies, gift stores, bookstores, art supplies, nurseries (the plant kind), useful things like hardware and bicycles, not especially useful things and a pile of miscellaneous stuff that we like.

First, here's an overview of some of the shopping areas.

Pleasant places to stroll and shop include:

- ◆ Lark Street in downtown Albany boasts small art and gift shops and little restaurants and coffee shops throughout.

- ◆ Delaware Avenue in downtown Albany also has a number of great food places and some up-and-coming gift shops.

+ River Street in Troy is the location of antique shops, art galleries, gift shops, and clothing stores, with great places to eat mixed in.

+ Saratoga, all of downtown. You could spend an entire day just browsing through the great collection of shops in downtown. The area features nice restaurants and a friendly bar district.

+ Jay Street, Schenectady, is divided into the pedestrian shopping end (the 100s) and North Jay where you will find Perreca's and Cornell's in Little Italy. Shopping on the pedestrian side is fun with an eclectic assortment of funkier stores and eateries.

+ Upper Union, Schenectady, is where you will find useful service shops mixed in with some little stores and Gershon's Deli.

+ Newtonville Plaza, Route 9, Newtonville, is the home of an assortment of specialty stores and restaurants, including a Bruegger's Bagels.

+ Remsen Street in Cohoes has a number of small places you can shop including Soft-Tex (the pillow place) and some very cozy coffeehouses. The New York State Wine Seller and The Bake Shop are located in the Harmony House Market Place.

The Malls

Crossgates is the monster mall with its huge Regal Crossgates Stadium 18 and IMAX theaters and hundreds of shops. Colonie Center is also pretty big—now with an L.L. Bean and Barnes and Noble, along with some new restaurants and a new Regal Cinema (with stadium seating). The Colonie Center shopping district extends east to west along Central Avenue and north along Wolf Road. Central Avenue, west of Albany, is a nonstop collection of strip malls. Northway Mall/Target Plaza is across Central Avenue from Colonie Center with a Target, Marshall's, Eddie Bauer's, JoAnn's Fabrics, and more, including a BJ's Wholesale Club and a Lowes. Stuyvesant Plaza is an open-air mall with smaller, quality shops including the wonderful Book House. Latham Circle Mall is the oldest in the area and almost empty, but J.C. Penney's is still there, as well as a Burlington Coat Factory Store, and a Lowes. There are plans for some kind of come back, but who knows when. Latham Farms, located close to Latham Circle off Route 7, contains Wal-Mart, Sam's Club, Home Depot, Dick's, and a Hannaford Grocery, along with a handful of other stores.

Now onto the details. We'll start with food!!

Food: Delis, Markets, Bakeries, and Sweets

Delis and Markets

There are grocery stores in every plaza around town that you can find on your own. This list contains specialty stores you might not have tried, but you should.

Aldi Store: 307 Columbia Turnpike, Rensselaer. This is a grocery store, but the prices are incredible. Most products are house brands, which are excellent and almost half the price of national brands. The produce is fresh and the frozen meals and packaged meats are quite good. It doesn't have everything, but it's worth the trip to save some real money.

Andy's: 256 Delaware Avenue, 463-2754. Walk into Andy's and you will want to eat everything in there. You can order big delicious sandwiches and Italian specialties to go; you will never have to cook again. The soups from Andy's grandma's recipes are so good and so filling, a small container and a piece of bread makes a complete meal.

Babushka Deli: 7 North Lake, Albany (near Western Avenue), 426-1499. Offering an authentic selection of specialty food from Russia and eastern Europe, the dark, dense, sour ryes are delicious and filling.

Cardona's Market: 340 Delaware Avenue, Albany, 434-4838. This is another great Italian deli/grocery that is just a short walk from the Spectrum. This market has everything; the store is bigger than you think and everything is fresh and delicious. They have great prepared foods, salads, more olives than you can imagine and extremely good help.

Delmar Marketplace: 406 Kenwood Avenue, Delmar, 439-3936, and McCarroll's The Village Butcher, 478-9651. Quality fresh meats and deli are the selections here. There is an excellent selection of prepared meals to heat at home, as well as a good organic and local food selection.

Genoa Importing: 435 Loudon Road, Loudonville, 427-0078. Quality imported foods can be found here, in addition to gourmet meals to take out, and fresh bread.

Halal Market: 264 Central Avenue, Albany, 426-4194. The market specializes in halal meat. There are several similar specialty stores in this area of Central Avenue.

Halal Meat and Grocery House of Spices: 638 Columbia Street Extension, Latham, 786-8229 (across from Latham Ford). Halal meats, spices, and groceries are sold here.

Honest Weight Food Coop: 484 Central Avenue, Albany, 482-2667. One of the great things you'll find in Albany. If you haven't been, you should go. There is a wide selection of fair-traded coffee beans that can be ground there or taken home for grinding. Bulk tofu that actually tastes good and tons of fresh organic foods can be purchased. The cheese selection is better than anywhere else. Everybody is nice here. GO!

India Bazaar: 1321 Central Avenue, Albany, 459-3108. This is a large Indian specialty market, and they have movies, too.

Kim's Oriental Shop: 1649 Central Avenue, Colonie, 869-9981. Kim's is a Korean, Chinese, and Japanese specialty food shop that includes sushi ingredients.

Lee's Asian Market: 1170 Central Avenue, Albany, 459-5250. This is the place to shop for Asian food specialties, including groceries, meat, seafood, and dry goods.

Ragonese Italian Imports: 409 New Scotland Avenue, Albany, 482-2358. Mediterranean gourmet foods can be bought here.

Rolf's Pork Store: 70 Lexington Avenue, Albany, 463-0185. This has been an Albany meat store for more than 140 years, and a German family-run one for four generations. The specialty meats are fresh and delicious. The German potato salad is the best anywhere and they carry a ton of German imports, including crossword puzzles, cookies, candy, and the best cough drops made with real fruit juice. Stop in, they are really friendly.

Roma Importing Co.: 9 Cobbee Road, Latham, 785-7480. Roma offers Italian food galore with great salads (the cole slaw is great). Cora mozzarella, which you can't buy in most groceries, is available here. They also have a pretty complete selection of the Twining loose teas in cans. Walk through the arch to get to the meat store featuring fresh, organic food.

Troy Community Food Coop: 77 Congress Street, Troy, 424-1131. Opening someday soon. It will be great when it does. Go to their Web: site www.troyfoodcoop.com for information or to join.

Uncle Sam's Natural Foods: 77 Fourth Street, Troy, 271-7299; 646 New Loudon Road, Latham, 782-5233. This is a great natural food store right in downtown Troy (and Latham, too) with a large selection of organic foods and products, including organic milk in glass bottles. The Troy store's sign with Uncle Sam is a hoot.

Bakeries

Bakeries. We love them. There's nothing quite like downing a few thousand calories of pure comfort. Here are a few, all with something special to offer.

The Bake Shop: 184 Remsen Street, Cohoes, 238-2232. Boasting a full lineup of home-baked goodies, which they will bake to order, this bakery also offers a small lunch menu of soups and signature sandwiches. The large orange/cranberry scones are delicious. Closed Sundays.

Bella Napoli: 672 New Loudon Road, Latham, 783-0196; 721 River Street, Troy, 274-8277. This is your full-service bakery, selling breads, pastries, rolls, donuts, specialty cookies, and cakes. The Latham store has a place to eat it all with some coffee. The mini elephant ears are especially delicious.

Bountiful Bread: 1475 Western Avenue, Stuyvesant Plaza, 438-3540. They feature a variety of great European-style breads with crispy crusts and wonderful, original sandwiches.

Bruegger's Bagels: 29 North Pearl Street, Albany; 55 Congress, Troy (many other locations, too). Yes, this is a chain, but a chain that started in 1983, in Troy. They have the best bagels in the country, maybe the world! The first Bruegger's is still located on Congress Street in Troy.

Cheesecake Machismo: 293 Hamilton Street, Albany, 427-7019. Buy a slice of homemade, delicious cheesecakes or, buy the whole thing and die happy. Changing specials mean you can come over and over again to find your new favorite.

Coccadott's Cake Shop: 1179 Central Avenue, Albany, 438-4937. Their specialty cakes are gorgeous and delicious, too. If you have your heart set on something memorable for your special day, they can make it.

Cookie Factory: 520 Congress Street, Troy, 268-1060. Only open for a couple of years, the Cookie Factory offers a familiar selection of Italian cookies and pastries. You can also find the Fudge Fancy doppelganger, the Fudge Fantasy here. The staff is friendly and helpful.

Dakota Steakhouse of Latham: Latham Farms, 579 Troy-Schenectady Road, Latham, 786-1234. Great steaks, but you can stop by and pick up some of their scrumptious buffalo, hearty grain bread to go.

Grandma's Country Pies and Restaurant: 1273 Central Avenue, Albany, 459-4585. Pies!

Joan's Cake Chateau: 285 Old Niskayuna Road, Latham, 783-6422. This little house of a cake shop has been turning out lovely special occasion cakes for at least 20 years. Let her bake you something special.

Perreca's Bakery: 33 N. Jay Street, Schenectady, 372-1875. Perreca's has the best Italian bread in the area.

Panera Bread Co: Everywhere, check the phonebook. Good, in house baked goods, but great soups and sandwiches to eat in or to go. Buy a whole brownie pie (not just a slice) and you'll be in heaven sooner.

The Placid Baker: 250 Broadway, Troy, 326-2657. The Placid Baker has moved his artisan breads, killer mudslide cookies and fabulous sticky buns to Troy. Hooray!!!!

Schuyler Bakery: 637 Third Avenue, Watervliet, 273-0142. This is a great little bakery with a large selection of very inexpensive baked goods. The crumb buns are a personal favorite.

Scratch Bakery Café: 452 Madison Avenue, Albany, 465-2233. We are fans of their chocolate cookies and they have a great selection of vegan snacks as well.

Sweet Treats Bakery: 28 Maple Avenue, Albany, 482-4084. Sweet Treats specializes in rye bread, and offers a small selection of pastries.

The Troy Waterfront Farmer's Market: The farmer's markets hosts several bread, cookie, and pastry bakers including Dutch Desserts (Kinderhook), Mrs. Londons (Saratoga), Our Daily Bread (Chatham), Placid Baker (Troy), and Ridvan (Niskayuna).

Villa Italia: 226 Broadway, Schenectady, 355-1144. The fancy Italian pastries (more than 40 mini varieties) here are beautiful to look at but better to eat. If you are in need of a wedding cake, they can make you one that's a work of art.

Zachary's Pastry Shoppe: 390 Columbia Turnpike, Rensselaer, 477-2140. The pastries here are almost too pretty to eat, but don't let that stop you—you won't be disappointed. They have a full selection of familiar and tasty standards and a lot of unusual and delectable others.

Orchards, Seasonal Pick Your Own

Altamont Orchards: 6654 Dunnsville Road, Altamont, 861-6515. The orchard features apples, a large farm stand, bedding plants, and donuts!

Bowman Orchards: 141 Sugar Hill Road, Rexford, 371-2042. Bowman grows dozens of varieties of apples including our favorites: galas and empires. Berry picking begins in June. Donuts and cider are available, too.

Devoe's Rainbow Orchard: 1569 Halfmoon Parkway (Route 9), Clifton Park. 371-8397.

Goolds Orchards: 1297 Brookview Station, Castleton, 732-7317. Apple Fest is always Columbus Day weekend and features music, crafts, local wine, and of course, apples.

Indian Ladder Farms: 342 Altamont Road, Altamont, 765-2956. Located at the base of the Helderbergs, you can enjoy the view as you pick apples, berries, or while shopping for fresh veggies. You can even get up close and personal to some real farm animals.

Lindsey's Idyllwood Orchard: 267 Sugar Hill Road, Rexford, 371-5785.

Riverview Orchards: 600 Riverview Road, Rexford, 371-2174. Although the apple picking is seasonal, the country store is open year-round. Apples and a donut robot that will make donuts right before your eyes.

Sweet Stuff

We are going to break this down into two of our favorites: ice cream and chocolate

I Scream, You Scream, We All Scream for Ice Cream

Because ice cream is so very important, here are the basic facts you need to know:

Gelato: Gelato is Italian ice cream made with milk, sugar, and flavorings. Eggs sometimes are added for stabilization. Gelato generally has less air than ice cream, giving a very smooth, dense consistency.

Ice cream (the hard-packed kind): Made with dairy products, sweeteners, and flavorings, it must have a minimum of 10% milk fat to be considered ice cream. The higher the fat content, the more delicious it tends to be. Ice cream has between 10% and 18% milk fat. The cooling method can have a drastic effect on how icy the ice cream tastes. One thing we didn't know is that a lot of ice cream has beef gelatin added for flavor and texture so vegetarians should ask before they indulge.

Sherbet/Sorbet: People tend to interchange these two, but sherbet can contain milk fat and has a sweet fruit flavoring, whereas sorbet should be nothing but frozen fruit puree.

Soft Serve Ice Cream: Invented by a chemical research team (mmmm yummy!), this was a way to double the amount of air in ice cream, thus cutting down on the cost of ingredients. The milk fat is lower, at 3% to 6%, but the air pumped through it makes it seem creamier. The air amount can be anywhere from 0% to 60%. The higher the amount of air, the quicker the ice cream melts. When it is overly pasteurized, it gets a waxy taste.

Now that you have the facts, you are ready to go get some ice cream. Here are a few of the best places to go. (Remember: Ice cream is seasonal and some of these places only are open during the warm months.)

Ben and Jerry's: 250 Lark Street, Albany, 463-7182. Ben and Jerry's opened its first ice cream store in 1978 with the idea that a business could be fair to its workers, suppliers, and the environment. In 2000, the company was sold to the multinational giant Unilever with the promise that the mission would remain the same. The ingredients, and much of the idealism, remain intact and you can still get really good ice cream there. In 2007, Ben and Jerry's has introduced Vanilla Toffee Crunch, which uses fair-traded ingredients. More flavors are headed in the same direction. They are open year-round, which is great for the ice cream lover in most of us.

Carvel Ice Cream & Bakery: 594 New Loudon Road, Latham, 785-4962. Carvel used to be the only place to get a soft, swirly cone of delicious ice cream. There aren't many Carvels around anymore, but some of the Price Choppers in town carry the Carvel brand. After a million years, Carvel is still making Fudgy the Whale and Cookie Puss ice cream cakes. It is, in a way, nice to still have something around that hasn't changed at all.

Cold Stone Creamery: Stuyvesant Plaza, 1475 Western Avenue, Albany, 514-2003. Cold Stone specializes in an ice cream that is midway between hard-packed and soft serve. Candy, nuts, and some flavorings are mixed in on a cold granite stone while you wait. A little pricey, but very good quality. It is open all year.

Crisan: 197 Lark Street, Albany, 445-2727. This is another great addition to the downtown. Crisan features wonderful gelato to savor by the cupful, as well as one of the best selections of pastries to go along with it.

Emack & Bolio's: 366 Delaware Avenue, Albany, 512-5100. This great place for ice cream opened in summer 2008, serving not only really creamy, delicious ice cream in 20 flavors (not all vegetarian, be sure to ask first), but wonderful brownies, cookies, and a selection of chocolates. Great location on Delaware, near the Spectrum Theaters.

Gelateria Lisa: 7 Hill Street in Troy's Little Italy, 883-6778. If you're missing "A Cone of Our Own" in Albany, these folks make some pretty delicious gelato as well. We've been working our way through all of the flavors and so far they are all fabulous. They serve up some nice lunches if you want to have real food first.

Guptill's Coney Express: 1085 New Loudon Road (Route 9), Cohoes, 785-0660. The best thing about this place is that it usually opens weeks before anybody else, so when you are desperately craving that first ice cream cone of the season, this is the place to go. The soft serve is good and creamy and the hard-packed ice cream comes in a multitude of flavors. Guptill's is located next to the roller rink if you need some fun exercise to work off those delicious calories.

Java Jazz Café: 318 Delaware Avenue, Delmar, 439-1727. This café offers Brown Cow, unbelievably creamy, organic ice cream in the basic flavors, with only a few specials. Brown Cow is probably the richest ice cream on the planet, so go and enjoy. Available year-round.

Kurver Kreme: 1349 Central Avenue, Albany, 459-4120. This has been a local favorite forever. The soft serve is good, although on a hot day it will melt before you reach your car. The pluses here are the variety of flavors and range of sizes and prices. They have a kids' cone that is just the right size and cheap!

Lickety Split: 589 Columbia Turnpike, East Greenbush, 477-9517. The soft serve here is a little waxy for our taste, but the variety of flavors and the hometown feel make this a popular tradition for local families. The Funplex is attached, making it a summertime destination.

Moxie's Ice Cream: 1344 Spring Avenue, Wynantskill, 283-4901. This place is really not that far out of Troy. Travel down Pawling Avenue and make a left on Spring Street. Moxie's is just a few miles down the road on the left, and definitely worth the trip. This is a family-run business that has been around for more than 40 years. Yes, there really is a Moxie, and yes, he knows how to make delicious ice cream. His daughter, Miss Pam, has been running the stand for the last 8 years. The ice cream is rich (15% milk fat) and the flavors are numerous. By the time National Ice Cream Day arrives (third Sunday in July) Moxie's has almost 70 different flavors including 5 different vanillas made from different beans from around the world. Moxie's is famous for its Blue Moon ice cream, an odd blue concoction of who knows what. In addition to great ice cream, the surrounding playground, with the best swings in the world, makes this place a treat in every way. Moxie's opens on Mother's Day. Spring hours are Monday through Friday, 3 to 9 p.m. and Saturday and Sunday from 1:30 to 9:30 p.m. Summer hours are everyday 1:30 to 9:30 p.m. They close for the season when the ice cream runs out, usually in late August.

On the Farm: 273 Troy-Schenectady Road, Latham, 785-9930. This has been a Latham summertime fixture for more than 23 years. They serve great soft serve in the basic varieties, with one special thrown in every couple of weeks. On the Farm serves Edy's hard-packed ice cream if you're not into the soft serve. They also have a lunch and dinner take-out menu (hamburgers, fish fry, french fries, etc.) that is pretty good. There are plenty of picnic tables. They sell Christmas trees here in late November.

The Peanut Principle: 1158 New Loudon Road, Cohoes, 783-8239. An in-season ice cream stand, it's their shakes that really bring in the crowds!

The Snowman: 531 Fifth Avenue, Troy, 233-1714. This is one of our favorites, mostly because of the weird snowman logo, but the tasty ice cream is home made and includes their own version of Blue Moon. The soft serve is smooth and thick. Although the parking lot doesn't offer the best ambience, you can walk down to the river near Melville's house and enjoy your ice cream there.

Stewart's Shops: All over. Yes, we're including Stewart's because their ice cream is actually good, available all year long, inexpensive, and everywhere. They even give it away on St. Patrick's Day if you wear green.

Toll Gate Ice Cream: 1569 New Scotland Road, Slingerlands, 439-9824. Family-run since 1949, Toll Gate sells delicious homemade ice cream. They serve food, too. Make this a tradition for your family.

Wholly Cow: 1836 Columbia Turnpike, Schodack, at the junction of routes 9 and 20. This place has creamy, thick soft-serve ice cream with a great taste. The flavors are just the basics, but all good. The big cones hold up in the summer heat. BBQ too!

Mmmmm Chocolate

And just so you can really appreciate it . . .

Cacao trees are certainly not native to this area, but surviving the upstate winters requires a certain amount (tonnage) of chocolate. Like ice cream, depending on the ingredients, chocolate can have a multitude of flavors. Chocolate was originally developed in Mexico and Central America from the cacao tree. Originally used to make some kind of bitter drink, the cacao seed also was fermented, dried, cleaned, and roasted. If you popped off the shell, you got the cacao nib, which was ground up to make chocolate liquor. Chocolate liquor could then be processed into cocoa solids and cocoa butter. (Chocolate with a high chocolate liquor content is usually better tasting.) Europeans fell in love with chocolate in the 1600s and tried developing cocoa plantations in their assorted colonies. This worked in western Africa where now 70% of the world's cocoa supply is grown.

Dark, bitter chocolate is pure cocoa solids and butter; milk chocolate adds the sugar and milk; and white chocolate (definitely a misnomer) has only the cocoa butter with no cocoa: basically, sugar and fat. Of the food we eat, chocolate has one of the higher concentrations of lead. We actually learned this by watching *CSI*, but Wikipedia backs it up. Apparently, the use of leaded gas mixed with acid rain, gets the lead in the cocoa beans in cocoa from Africa. But hey, you also get a bunch of antioxidants in dark chocolate and cocoa also has been shown to lower blood pressure and increase blood flow. Thanks to the recession of the 1990s and corporate America's need to consume smaller companies, some of the best suppliers of really delicious chocolate have been gobbled up and their original recipes ruined. And even though we think chocolate really has changed for the worst in the past number of years, and although locally, it can cost between $12 and $40 a pound, we are totally addicted. Here are some nearby sources.

Aldi Store: 307 Columbia Turnpike, East Greenbush. Yes, we know this is a grocery store but it's a German-owned store that imports a lot of delicious German products including chocolate. You can get huge bars of it here for about $4 per pound. The fruit and nut bar they carry is great. It contains hazelnuts, rather than peanuts, with sweet raisins in a very good chocolate. If chocolate is your main food group, you might want to try some here and save a ton of money at the same time.

Café Deli-icious: 413 River Street, Troy, 271-8787. The selection here includes gift baskets, fancy fruit platters, and really yummy chocolate-dipped strawberries.

Candyland Confectionery: 574 Columbia Turnpike, East Greenbush, 477-9444. This is the place to buy all your make-it-at-home chocolate supplies. They have the melting chocolate, molds, and books—a large selection of everything you need to get started.

Chocolate Gecko: 21 Colvin Avenue, Albany, 436-0866 (also available at Laurel's Flowers, 540 Delaware Avenue). Chocolate Gecko uses only natural, organic ingredients and produces a very nice selection of beauti-ful-looking chocolates. The flavors are more subtle and sophisticated and quite delicious. They are sold by the piece, so at $1.50 each you can't really overdose without breaking the bank. The Colvin Avenue location offers offer classes in chocolate making, which is a nice addition to Albany.

Emack & Bolio's: 366 Delaware Avenue, Albany, 512-5100. Yes, this is an ice cream place AND a chocolate shop. They offer a limited but surprisingly good selection. Their turtles have peanuts rather than the traditional pecans, but are still very tasty. The store covers all of the bases here, with excellent ice cream, chocolate, a case of delicious baked goods (cookies, brownies), and assorted beverages.

Isn't It Sweet: 575 New Scotland Avenue, 489-9820. Handmade chocolates and confections, this shop is located across from St. Peter's Hospital.

Krause's Homemade Candy: 1609 Central Avenue, Albany, 869-3950. This is an Albany mainstay. The store is bright, cheerful, and just the right place to find a delicious gift. We really like their milk chocolate turtles and caramels, but find the flavor of some of their creams to be too overwhelming. Prices are at the lower end of the spectrum, which means you can indulge in some excellent chocolate without having to give up food for a week, although living on nothing but chocolate has a certain appeal.

The Peanut Principle: 1158 New Loudon Road, Cohoes, 783-8239, near Guptill's. Although this store has a pretty decent selection of chocolate, the flavorings are really too strong for our taste. The caramels are smooth and creamy with a taste you'd expect. However, the nuts are what you come here for. There is a large selection of many varieties and flavorings that make the trip here worthwhile. They also serve ice cream and shakes in the summer only. The shakes are one of the best around.

Uncle Sam's Candy: 2571 Albany Street, Schenectady, 372-2243. We like Uncle Sam's a lot. The store carries a very large assortment of handmade chocolate (including sugar free). Their creams are not over the top flavored like some, but instead, are really good, as are their caramels. Their assorted chocolate barks are especially delicious. The best thing here is the enormous selection of chocolates molded into almost any shape you can imagine, from cats to dogs to electronics to tools and farm animals. It comes in milk, dark, and white chocolate. Uncle Sam's also has the best licorice in town.

Wine and Spirits

All Star Wine and Spirits: 579 Troy-Schenectady Road, Latham Farms, Latham, 220-9463. This is a wine superstore with such an enormous selection from all over the world, you can browse forever. All price ranges are available. The employees know their wines and are very helpful with good suggestions.

Empire Wine and Liquor: 1440 Central Avenue, in the Northway Mall, Colonie, 694-8503. We like this place. It has great prices on the standards and a pretty good wine selection. We have tried some of the $5 imports, which were surprisingly good.

New York State Wine Seller at Harmony House Marketplace: 190 Remsen Street, Cohoes, 238-2232. This lovely shop carries wine from 125 of New York's 260 vineyards. Wine tasting is every Friday from 5 to 7 p.m. and features a different winery each week. You can get answers to all of your burning wine questions straight from the winemakers.

Wine Shop: 265 New Scotland Road, Albany, 438-1116. This is one of the great little places in Albany. There's no need to have your own wine cellar when you can find an extraordinary selection of wines from all over and in all price ranges right here. The staff is knowledgeable and helpful.

Useful Things You Will Need

Hardware Stores

A. Philips Hardware Inc.: 292 Central Avenue, Albany, 465-8861 (and throughout the area). Phillips Hardware is a small chain based in Albany, whose focus is on service. The Central Avenue location is the closest hardware store for downtown residents. Even so, it is a real hardware store with all of the stuff you need to fix all of the broken stuff you have. They also make keys.

Carr Hardware (formerly De Lollo's): 701 19th Street, Watervliet, 274-7019. The friendliest hardware store you'll find, despite the recent change in ownership. The store has almost everything and if they don't, they can probably get it for you.

Pfeil Hardware: 63 Third Street, Troy, 687-0014. If a bright, beautiful hardware store makes you swoon, stop in and visit this two floor, chock-full delight.

Nerdland
(With apologies to Weather Report.)

Computer Supplies and Parts

You can get new games and gaming systems at the major chains (look in the phonebook) or at some of the local shops like Flights of Fantasy or EB Games. But for your computer needs, the following list contains places you can go for expert help and that odd component for an older system.

Abi Computer Inc.: 90 Hoosick Street, Troy, 270-9933. This is a small retail and repair shop with new, new-in-box older, and used components and a knowledgeable and friendly owner.

A&G Computers: 614 19th Street, Watervliet, 274-5123. This is a small shop with retail parts and repair for mostly older systems.

Computer Renaissance: 595 New Loudon Road, Latham, 220-4445. This is a retail and repair shop with an emphasis on customer service and newer systems and supplies (www.comprenny.com).

eLot Electronics Recycling: 8000 Main Street (in the industrial park), Troy, 266-9385. "Recycle. Reuse. Recover." Don't' discard your old mercury light bulbs, batteries, and electronics in a landfill—they generate toxic waste—eLot recovers and reuses as much as possible. The store has a large used component selection including motherboards priced from $10, desktop systems from $59, and LCD monitors from $75.

Technology Surplus Superstore: Building 405 Scotia-Glenville Industrial Park, Route 5, Scotia, 377-2200. Not quite what you'd expect going by its name, this small warehouse store has some good deals on a variety of systems and great prices on flat-screen monitors. They also run an electronics recycling program (www.techsurplusstore.com).

Electronics: Parts and Supplies

Grimmer's Electric Supply: 41 Brandywine Avenue, Schenectady, 374-8480. Grimmer's is an old-fashioned electronics supply store with a tube tester.

Trojan Electronic Supply: 15 Middleburg Street, Troy, 274-448.1 The store looks like an old barn on the outside and it is one on the inside, but electronics nerds swoon when they enter this parts and components retail store/museum. Do you need a No. 49 2V flashlight bulb? Try finding it on the Web. Trojan Electronic Supply has it. Do you need a brand new LCD oscilloscope? They've got that too.

Bicycle Shops

CK Cycles (formerly Klarsfeld's Cyclery and Fitness): 1370 Central Avenue, Albany, 459-3272. This shop has been around forever. They know bikes and have a high-quality selection of bikes and accessories.

Downtube Cycle Shop: 466 Madison Avenue, Albany (across from Washington Park), 434-1711. Great bikes for the whole family and really friendly service. Look for the nice box of bells behind the counter.

Freemans Bridge Sports, Inc.: 38 Freemans Bridge Road, Scotia, 382-0593 (just over the bridge from Schenectady). This is a serious bike shop for the serious rider, with a great selection of bicycles and accessories.

Plaine's Bike Ski Snowboard: 1816 State Street, Schenectady, 346-1433. Plaine's boasts a LARGE, full-service shop.

Rudy's Schwinn Cyclery Bike Shop: 578 Second Avenue, Troy, 235-2525. This is a small place with a good selection of road and mountain bikes and accessories to go with them. Rudy's has a repair service, too!

Sycaway Bicycle Sales and Service: 13 Lord Avenue (off Hoosick Street), Troy, 273-7788. This is a really friendly shop with a selection of better bicycles. As the name says: Service for your broken bicycles as well.

Repair and Recycle Bikes

Bike Rescue: This is a volunteer-run bicycle resource center where you can get help fixing your bike or get connected with one that needs adopting. In Troy, 51 Third Street; Albany, 15 Trinity Place basement (near Madison). Contact troybikerescue.org

Concept Bikes: 528-1668. Michael Vincent runs this bike repair shop out of his truck. He has everything required to fix your broken bicycle on the road and he makes house calls.

Clothing

Aurora's Boutique: 11 Third Street, Troy, 266-1191. Upscale women's clothing (mostly formal wear), this boutique features styles by Ursula of Switzerland, lovely jewelry, and accessories.

Capital Kidzwear: 204 Washington Avenue, Albany, 462-2791. Urban kids' clothes at affordable prices can be purchased here.

Fancy Schmancy: 1800 Western Avenue, Albany, 452-1269. If you go a short distance out of town, you will be surprised to find a store tucked into a nondescript strip mall that carries a large selection of beautiful, feminine clothing, gorgeous costume jewelry, and hats that would make Mary Lou Whitney jealous.

Lodge's-Albany's Oldest Store: 75 North Pearl Street, Albany, 463-4646. You have to go, just because. You can find items you didn't know they still made, along with everything else.

Lollipops: 594 New Loudon Road, Latham, 786-0379. The kids' clothes here are so cute you'll want them in your size. This is where you drag grandma to buy something special for her precious grandchildren.

Some Girls Boutique: 17 Colvin Avenue, Albany, 489-0505 and **Some Girls Troy,** 13 Second Street, Troy, 271-1172. At both of these shops you will find trendy women's clothes and accessories without having the hassle of going to the mall. These are fun stores to shop in.

Sweater Venture: 700 Columbia Turnpike, East Greenbush, 477-9317. Not just sweaters—although they have an amazing selection of hand-knit sweaters from around the world—but also jewelry, gifts, the funkiest of hats, gloves, scarves, and the nicest store cat in the area. This store is well worth the short trip. They have special sales throughout the year during which you can get some great deals.

Truly Rhe: 11 Second Street, Troy, 273-1540. This is a beautiful shop with lovely women's clothing and accessories, ranging from casual to elegant.

WynCrest Farm: 19 Great View Terrace, Voorheesville, 475-7774. Although this is not a store, we bought a pair of the alpaca socks at one of the local farmer's markets and they are amazing. They are super soft and warm and come in beautiful heathery colors. The owner will mail you a pair from her farm (www.alpacasandllamas.com).

Furniture Stores

Huck Finn's Warehouse: 25 Erie Boulevard, Albany, 465-3373. This is a big place with lots of merchandise to choose from and the best carpet selection around.

Kincaid Home Furnishings: 801 New Loudon Road, Latham, 783-1850. Kincaid features high-end, absolutely gorgeous furniture that will hold up for generations.

Kugler's Red Barn: 425 Consaul Road, Colonie, 370-2468. This is a furniture store that's actually in a red barn and sells solid, country, shaker styles made by small quality companies right here in the United States.

Mooradian's Furniture: 800 Central Avenue, Albany, 489-2529. In business for 75 years, this store carries a full line of furniture for the whole house at good prices and they offer quick delivery, too.

New Old Stuff: 615 Pawling Avenue, Troy, 274-3221. Featuring American-made solid wood furniture with a lovely antique look, this store has a large selection of unusual home accessories and its own sweet shop.

Old Brick: 2910 Campbell Road, Schenectady, 377-1600; 33-37 Warehouse Row (on Railroad Avenue), Albany, 438-9600; 2 River Street,

Troy, 273-2000. Old Brick sells solid, beautiful furniture—the kind you can pass down to the next generation—at great prices.

Taft Furniture: 1960 Central Avenue, Albany, 456-3361. This is a huge furniture store/warehouse—hey it is "the big store"—with everything you need for your home.

Antique, Thrift, and Retro Sources

Bournebrook Antique Center: 172 River Street, Troy, 273-3027. These guys keep the most regular hours and have a huge selection of all kinds of stuff, including a good collection of antique jewelry, lighting, china, furniture, and all kinds of collectibles from assorted vendors.

Community Closet Thrift Shop: 158 Remsen Street, Cohoes. Here you'll find clothing and household items all at a price YOU set. The shop is open Tuesdays 1 to 4 p.m., Thursdays 10 a.m. to 4 p.m., and until 7 p.m. on the second Tuesday of each month.

Coxsackie Antique Center: 12400 State Route 9W, West Coxsackie, 731-8888. The antique center features items from more than 100 dealers. Shopping here is more fun than you can imagine and they have everything. It is open 7 days a week from 10 a.m. to 8 p.m.

For Pete's Sake "A Thrifty Place": 583 New Scotland Avenue, Albany (corner of South Allen and New Scotland), 525-1107. Connected with St. Peter's Hospital, this shop offers nice, usually upscale clothing.

Goodwill: 720 Hoosick Street, Troy, 272-8451. This is the Goodwill superstore, carrying lots of new, discontinued, and used clothing. It is open daily.

Goodwill: 1 Fuller Road, Albany, 459-5580. Goodwill stores don't seem to have quite the eclectic selection that Salvation Army has, but offers weekly specials for everyone. Goodwill is open on Sunday and all of the half price items from the previous week are discounted even further.

Great Finds: 260 Washington Avenue, Albany, 449-7715. Hats and gently used clothing for women can be purchased here at low prices. The shop is open weekdays and late for First Fridays.

Jermain Thrift Shop: 601 Fifth Avenue, Watervliet, in the Jermain Church Gym, 273-8220. This thrift shop offers a nice selection of clothing and items for your home at unbelievable prices. It is open Tuesday and Friday from 10 a.m. to 1:30 p.m. and the first and third Saturday of each month from 10 a.m. to 1 p.m.

Leisure Time Flea Market: 2532 Route 9W, Ravena, 756-8772. This is a little out of the way, but it's a year-round indoor flea market that is always a fun experience. The Coxsackie Antique Center is just a few miles down the road on the left, just past the thruway entrance.

Living Room: 274 River Street, Troy, 266-9311. Elizabeth Young runs this great store for quality antique furniture and great retro pieces. Over at 78 Fourth Street, her parents run Antiek, an enormous warehouse of antique furniture and accessories.

Liz's Closet: 1762 Western Avenue, Albany, 452-1001. This is a consignment shop with better-quality clothes at good prices.

Metropolis Vintage: 32 Fuller Road, Albany, 438-8277. This is where you get the vintage dress of your dreams and the fabulous jewelry to go with it. The cooler kind of antiques as well.

Niskayuna Antiques (used to be White House Flea Market): 3901 State Street, Schenectady, 346-7851. A very long time ago, this shop was located in an actual white house in downtown Schenectady, however, it has moved a few times and is now in the old Duanes Toyland store. Antiques and collectibles from 40 vendors are all inside; good hours.

Opus Igor: 260 Lark Street, Albany, 396-5360. Featuring work from local artists and crafters, this is a relatively new consignment shop.

Pete's Place: 444 River Street, Troy, 892-6023. Pete is there everyday and his large downstairs store has everything you need with the exception of clothing. His merchandise changes weekly and he usually has a good selection of bicycles, house wares, electronics, appliances, furniture, tools, and even LPs.

Plato's Closet: 818 Central Avenue, Albany, 459-3104. This is the place to buy and sell used teen/junior clothing.

Ravena Barn Sales Flea Market and Thrift Shop: Route 9W, Ravena (1/4 mile south of the Ravena traffic light), 756-7778. A whole lot of everything, this establishment is open 7 days a week from 10 a.m. to 4 p.m.

Salvation Army: 452 Clinton Avenue, Albany, 465-2416; 350 Troy-Schenectady Road, Latham, 783-7120. The Latham location has a pretty interesting selection of merchandise and discounts certain tags during the week. At the Latham store, Tuesday is half price day for seniors and Wednesday is half price day for everyone, but parking is a bear on that day.

Something Olde Something New: 1969 New Scotland Road, Slingerlands, 475-0663. This shop offers better secondhand clothing and a good selection of furniture and décor stuff at good prices.

Treasure Chest Thrift Shop: 295 Hamilton, Albany, 436-7451. Proceeds from purchases you make here go to the Damien Center, which helps those living with AIDS and HIV. The shop offers a nice selection of clothing and house wares.

The Trojan Horse: 282B River Street, Troy, 270-5146. Adding to the already nice collection of antique stores in downtown Troy is the Trojan Horse. There are some beautiful pieces here.

Twilight: 44 Fourth Street, Troy, 326-2211. Go upstairs to this vintage clothing store to find some pretty cool stuff. They have evening hours, Monday and Wednesday through Friday 3 to 8 p.m. and Saturday, 10 a.m. to 6 p.m., but are always open for Troy Night Out, which is the last Friday of every month.

Vintage Options: 205 River Street, Troy, 272-2083. With its ever-changing selection of vintage clothing and collectibles, this shop is a real blast from the past.

For the Dogs (and Cats and Other Creatures, Too)

Benson's Pet Center: 197 Wolf Road, Albany, 435-1738. Benson's supplies everything your pet needs, including food, toys, and medications.

Davey Jones Locker: 386 Delaware Avenue, Albany, 436-4810. Everything your scalier variety of pet could need is here.

Eddie's Aquarium Center: 1254 New Loudon Road, Latham, 783-3474 (783-FISH). The staff at Eddie's is expert in the fish and reptile worlds. The store has everything you could possibly need.

Healthy Pet Center: 237 North Greenbush Road, Troy, 283-4027. This store features a great selection, friendly service, and a tank of mesmerizing live coral.

Oz Professional Pet Sitters: PO Box 542, East Greenbush, 542-6814, e-mail them at OzPetsitters@nycap.rr.com. They will take care of your babies at home. We know them, they love all animals, and will love yours, too.

Pearl's Pet Food and Supplies: 243 Delaware Avenue, Delmar, 439-9933. Friendly, knowledgeable staff and a good selection of merchandise can be found here.

PetSmart: 609 Troy-Schenectady Road, Latham Farms, Latham, 785-4621. This is your full-service pet superstore and they have everything, including adoption clinics from local shelters.

Pet Supplies Plus: 1235 Western Avenue, Albany, 438-1040. One of the places for great selection and prices.

Bookstores

The national chains, Barnes and Noble and Borders, are locally represented in the malls. Privately owned shops continue to serve readers who
are looking for unusual and used books.

The Book Barn: 200 Troy-Schenectady Road, Latham, 786-1368. With
more than 100,000 used books, you can browse here for hours. The
largest selection is in popular titles, including romances and mysteries.
The owner stocks a pretty large section of books on military history, as
well.

The Book House: 1475 Western Avenue, Stuyvesant Plaza, Albany,
489-4761. These are the same people who own Market Block Books in
Troy. They love books and it shows. The Little Book House is ideal for
children with some really sweet children's books.

Dove & Hudson: 296 Hudson Avenue at the corner of Dove and Hudson, Albany, 432-4518. This is the best used bookstore in all the land.
We want to read everything in here. Go. Go now!

Friar Tuck Newsroom and Tobacconist: 180 Delaware Avenue, Delmar,
439-3742 (there is a Friar Tuck at the Rensselaer train station as well).
This is a huge store with more than 5,000 magazines, tons of books,
and cigarettes and cigars.

I Love Books: 380 Delaware Avenue, Delmar, 478-0715. This shop
offers a moderate selection of new books, as well as cards and gifts.

Lyrical Ballad Bookstore: 7 Phila Street, Saratoga, 584-8779. Nonfic-
tion, art, and antiquarian books can be found in a labyrinth of an old

bank. If you can't find that rare book you've been looking for, it just might be here.

Market Block Books: 290 River Street, Troy, 328-0045. This store is a nice addition to Troy's downtown, offering a good selection and a great browsing atmosphere.

Mary Jane Books: 215 Western Avenue, Albany, 465-2238. You don't browse here, you just bring your textbook list and they will get it for you. They buy and sell thousands of college texts efficiently and painlessly.

M.O.S.S. Books: 51 Congress Street, Troy, 274-0199. The Russell Sage Bookstore attached to Bruegger's Bagels has textbooks upstairs and a current-release bookstore and gift shop downstairs.

Open Door Bookstore: 128 Jay Street, Schenectady, 346-2719. This is a really nice bookstore, where you feel right at home right away and can find books you want just inside the doors. They also carry a good selection of better fun gifts.

Comic Book Stores

Aquilonia: 412 Fulton Street, Troy, 271-1069. This is the best comic book store on Earth, near Troy.

Earthworld: 537 Central Avenue, Albany, 459-2400. The other best comic book store on Earth, near Albany.

Excellent Adventures Comics & Collectibles: 110 Milton Avenue, Ballston Spa, 884-9498. We know this is a little out of town, but these guys have a ton of great old comic books at really good prices.

Creative Supplies

AC Moore Inc.: 873 New Loudon Road, Latham, 782-0095. If you just don't know what to do with your spare time, you can certainly find some little project to work on in here. They don't really specialize in one specific craft area, but you can probably find something close to what you need.

Albany Art Room: 457-Madison Avenue, Albany, 427-3910. Art supplies and books are available in the store, but the Albany Art Room also offers art classes and/or work space for artists at all levels.

Alfred's Fabric Center: 1814 Central Avenue, Kohl's Plaza, 456-6700. Alfred's can still surprise you with a great find from New York, something the chains can't get for you. And they know what white spandex is without having to look up a sku number for it.

Arlene's Artist Materials, Inc.: 57 Fuller Road, Albany, 482-8881. Yes, this is a great art supply store and fun to just walk around in to see what you didn't know you needed; however, it also has a great selection of postcards and greeting cards, which are a lot less boring than the grocery store variety.

Central Art Supply: 292 Lark Street, Albany, 426-3501. This small shop carries what you need and offers a student discount.

JoAnn's Fabrics: 1440 Central Avenue, in the Northway Mall, Albany, 459-5026. One of the last fabric stores in the area, JoAnn's carries lots of fleece, dress-up fabrics, and quilting supplies. The home décor fabrics are pretty good as well. The craft department is limited but OK.

Hill's Stationery: 451 Broadway, Troy, 274-1080. Office, art, and drafting supplies can be found on the shelves here.

Miller Paint and Decorating: 296 Central Avenue, Albany, 465-1526. The set designers we know love Miller for supplies. They should know.

Northeast Ceramic Supply: 621 River Street, Troy, 274-2722. All the supplies you need for ceramics, including kilns, glazes, green ware, and molds, can be found here.

Stampassion Ltd.: 595 New Loudon Road, Newton Plaza, Latham, 782-7227. Stampassion stocks tons of rubber stamps and all the supplies you need to go with them.

Nurseries and Greenhouses

Capital District Cooperative, Inc.: 381 Broadway, Menands, 465-1023. Drive around back behind the hardware store to find Esposito, Decker's

Produce, and others offering bedding and other plants at wholesale prices. This is a great place to get the plants you need to start your garden.

Faddegon's Nursery, Inc.: 1140 Troy-Schenectady Road, Latham, 785-6726. The nursery features a large selection of all types of trees and shrubs with a knowledgeable staff. They also can design your garden for you.

George's Market & Nursery: 240 Wade Road, Extension, across from Target, Latham, 783-3474. Now in its fabulous new location, George's continues to offer a huge selection of annuals, perennials, trees, shrubs, garden supplies, and gifts—all at great prices. The staff is very friendly and helpful.

Troy's Landscape Supply: 1266 New Loudon Road (Route 9), Cohoes, 785-1526. Offering a huge and unusual selection of plants, shrubs, and trees on 25 acres, Troy's Landscape also carries tools, rocks, and paving stones to help you design the perfect garden.

Valoze Greenhouses, Inc.: 5 Grove Lane (Route 9) Cohoes, 785-4343. Thousands of beautiful bedding plants are available in season.

Post Offices

Albany: 45 Hudson Avenue, 25 Eagle Street, 240 State Street, 1226 Broadway, 747 Broadway (annex), 71 Terminal Street, 332 Delaware Avenue, 563 New Scotland Avenue, 450 Central Avenue, 475 Albany-Shaker Road.

Colonie Center: 1425 Central Avenue, second floor of Colonie Center near Boscovs.

Troy: The big one is at 400 Broadway.

Latham: 685 Watervliet-Shaker Road.

Newtonville: 552 Loudon Road. This post office is listed on the National Register of Historic Places.

Watervliet: 145 16th Street.

Musical Instruments

Cathedral Music: 1813 Fifth Avenue, Troy, 273-5138. Specializing in quality handcrafted acoustic guitars from around the world, this is for the really serious guitar player who also appreciates a true work of art. Expert repair also is offered.

Coles Woodwind Shop: 360 Broadway, second floor, Saratoga, 450-0333. Normally we wouldn't send you this far out of town, but Bill Cole has saved more than one of our trumpets from becoming a bugle. He specializes in high-end wind instruments.

Daddy's Junky Music: 1770 Central Avenue, Albany, 452-9431. We purchased a pretty nice guitar from their used department. It is worth the stop if you are shopping around.

Drome Sound: 3905 State Street, Schenectady, 370-3701. This store has been around for a long time and we're always amazed that they can find the missing pieces to one of our musical instruments in one of their "boxes-o-stuff." Friendly and knowledgeable musicians work here.

Guitar Center: 145 Wolf Road, Albany, 446-1500. The big box store of pop music instruments, the Guitar Center offers a great selection and great prices. You can check all of the prices online before you get there.

Hermie's Music Store: 727 State Street, Schenectady, 374-7433. The State Street store has a great selection of all types of instruments. They can repair that old clarinet you found in the attic, or build you the drum kit of your dreams.

John Keal Music Co.: 819 Livingston Street, Albany, 482-4405. Band instruments can be purchased or rented here; band equipment and sheet music is for sale.

L.A.'s Hilton Music Center: Colonie Center on Wolf Road, Albany, 459-9400. The offerings here are mostly drums and guitars. Good lessons are available.

Northeast Music: 885 New Loudon Road, Latham, 783-1658. Northeast provides quality concert band instruments and repair.

Parkway Music: 1602 Route 9, Clifton Park, 383-0300. Chock full of new and used instruments, amplifiers, and vintage items, this is a fun place to shop.

Segel Violins: 44 Third Street, Troy, 266-9732. Segal Violins specializes in high-quality instruments and sheet music, as well as expert repairs.

Schenectady Van Curler Music: 432 State Street, Schenectady, 374-5318. This is your source for NYSSMA sheet music. If you don't know what NYSSMA (New York State School Music Association) is, you don't belong here.

Used Vinyl and CDs

The Beat Shop: 197 River Street, Troy, 272-0433. Specializing in new and used, local and obscure music, the shop features frequent live performances, vinyl LPs, CDs, movies, and posters.

Blue Note Record Shop: 156 Central Avenue, Albany, 462-0221. This classic music shop specializes in vinyl LPs and 45s and a great jazz collection.

Last Vestige: 173 Quail, Albany, 432-7736. Thousands of records in every genre are in stock.

Jewelry and Gifts

The Broken Mold Studio: 284 River Street, Troy, 273-6041. A number of different artists have created the lovely selection of pottery found in this studio.

The Counties of Ireland: 77 Third Street, Troy, 687-0054. This store contains a beautiful collection of sweaters, scarves, jewelry, and accessories, as well as food specialties imported from Ireland.

Elissa Halloran Designs: 225 Lark Street, Albany, 432-7090. Elissa features original jewelry in this beautiful new store. This is where you can get a WOW gift.

Eye Candy: 188 River Street, Troy, 272-9550. The "eye candy" here is beautiful, handmade jewelry.

Frank Adams Jewelers: 1475 Western Avenue, Stuyvesant Plaza, Albany, 435-0075. This is a family-run, *very* fine jewelry store where you can certainly find the perfect gift.

JK Bloom Jewelers: 21 Third Street, Troy, 272-1807 Diamond jewelry, including engagement rings are made right in the store. The designers can create just the ring you were hoping for.

Mayfair Jewelers: 549 Troy-Schenectady Road, Latham, 785-7898 (next to Starbucks). Mayfair carries a full selection of gold, diamonds, watches, and flatware. They also have done some really good repair work for us on some old pieces.

The Paper Sparrow: 288 River Street, Troy, 272-7227. Merchandise here includes some funky, local and imported jewelry, cards, food, gifts, bags, clothing, cute baby stuff, and a variety of framed art. The gallery space in the back room features frequently changing exhibits.

Philip Alexander Jewelers: 475 Albany-Shaker Road, Loudonville, 438-6350. This store has estate jewelry, lots of it, and gives appraisals.

Prism Glass Works: 2303 15th Street, Troy, 273-8556. Brightly colored, funky, hand-blown glass pipes, goblets, jewelry, and marbles can be purchased here. They give lessons, too. They are open weekdays noonish until eightish.

River Rocks Jewelry and Bead Shop: 209-211 River Street, Troy, 273-4532. River Rocks offers a huge selection of beautiful glass, silver, and gemstone beads with all the supplies you need to put them together. The shop sells one-of-a-kind designer jewelry and some gift items from around the world. They are closed Mondays.

Romanation Jewelers: 48 Third Street, Troy, 272-0643. Romanation offers a large selection of fine jewelry and watches, as well as a very good selection of antique and estate jewelry.

Romeo's: 299 Lark Street, Albany, 434-4014. Romeo's carries a bunch of very cool everything, including vintage clothing, home décor, jewelry, cards, gifts, and a full line of massage oils and more.

Science and Hobby: 1632 Second Avenue, Watervliet, 272-9040. This is an extensive hobby store that is stocked with everything from balsa wood to telescopes and RC cars. The most impressive part of the store is the huge RC racetrack with ramps and jumps. RC and nitro car enthusiasts gather on Sundays from October to March to race and show off. "Commentators" are welcome.

Silver Birch Trading Post: 294 Delaware Avenue, Albany, 439-0724. A wide variety of gifts and local art can be purchased here.

The Spinning Seed: 272 River Street, Troy, 268-1499. A store that sells things good for you and the planet, whether its fair-traded, organic, recycled, or recyclable, its all here for you, your kids, and your pets.

Galleries

Albany Center Gallery: 39 Columbia Street, Albany, 462-4775. A rich 30-year history now in new digs, the gallery offers a great place to see some of the outstanding, creative work by local artists.

The Arts Center of the Capital Region: 265 River Street, Troy, 273-0552. In the last few years, this arts center has really begun to shine. The shows are well curated and worth spending some real time looking at. The center offers dozens of classes and holds performances in the Joseph L. Bruno Theater. Start enjoying it at Troy Night Out.

Clement Art Gallery: 201 Broadway, Troy, 272-6811. This gallery features changing monthly exhibits that focus on local artists, as well as a large selection of matted art and expert framing.

Fulton Street Gallery: 406 Fulton Street, Troy, 274-8464. Run solely by volunteers, this gallery focuses on local artists.

Martinez Gallery: 3 Broadway, Troy, 274-9377. This is another of the galleries in Troy that we like a lot. The gallery focuses mostly on Latino and Latin American art and every show is exciting. If you are not able to afford one of the installed pieces, there are nice prints and unframed pieces that are definitely affordable.

Photocenter—The Photography Center of the Capital District: 404 River Street, Troy, 273-0100. As well as offering gallery space to its members, the Photocenter has studio space and equipment for use by its members to pursue all aspects of photography. Basic membership begins at $35 per year (www.photocentertroy.org).

Upstate Artists Guild (UAG): 247 Lark Street, Albany, 426-3501. Exhibiting the art of more than 250 artists and administering Albany's First Fridays, UAG brings art to the masses. The guild hosts monthly gallery exhibitions as well as different workshops. You can and should become a member and support the arts in Albany (www.upstateartisisguild.org).

Miscellany

This stuff doesn't fit any category in particular, but you might need some of it sometime. In no particular order (except alphabetical):

Ada's Spirit Works: 328 Delaware Avenue, Albany, 436-8282. This is the place to go for readings and spiritual supplies and an enormous selection of candles to put just the right spell on whomever you want.

Albany Theater Supply: 445 N. Pearl Street, Albany, 465-8895. Exactly. Need blackout cloth. It's here.

Alpro Antique & Lighting: 227 Lark Street, Albany, 434-3363. So the Queen is coming for a visit and you want to spiff up the manor and get the old chandelier up and running; they can do that for you here.

Bob's Trees: 1227 W. Galway Road, Hagaman 882-9455. If you want to cut your own "holiday" tree you can do it here or just pick up a fresh cut one. All kinds of trees can be found here. Great smells with a nice place to warm up with a cup of hot cocoa, Bob's may be far, but it's definitely worth the trip.

Capital Costumes: Second floor, Crossgates Mall next to the Food Court, 456-5754. This is a great place to find a full range of costumes.

The Costumer: 1995 Central Avenue, Albany, 464-9031, and their original store at 1020-1030 Barrett Street, Schenectady, 374-7442. Costumes for purchase or for rent this is a fun place to buy a gift for that hard-to-shop-for person.

Franklin Plaza: Fourth and Grand streets, Troy, 270-9622. Planning a grand party and have no idea where to hold it? The Franklin Plaza just might be your answer. Located in an old banking building (the cloak room is the old vault), this establishment has a comfortable elegance and serves fabulous food. The building dates back to 1833 but was completely restored in 1992. The ballrooms are gorgeous and the staff is very friendly and accommodating.

The Gas Menagerie: 1627 Fifth Avenue, Troy, 272-3087. Got a Jag or Range Rover that needs to be repaired? Patrick O'Reilly runs this one-man show from his small garage in Troy and with 30-plus years experience, he's one of the few who knows what he's doing and can expertly fix up your baby.

Happy Ice LLC: 2 Commerce Avenue, Albany, 438-2070. Dry ice!!!!!!

Historic Albany Foundation's Architectural Parts Warehouse: 89 Lexington Avenue, Albany, 465-2987. Missing doors, windows, plumbing parts, mantles, etc. for your old house? You might be able to find them here. Donations of historic house parts in good shape are accepted as well.

Infamous Graphics: 1033 Central Avenue, Albany, 459-7446. Full graphic and Web design services are offered and if you want to turn your car into a rolling billboard, these guys can give it a full color vehicle wrap.

Lexington Vacuum: 997 Central Avenue, Albany, 482-4427. When you need the odd belt, hose, or bag, this is the place to go. They also do repairs.

Orion Boutique: 169 Jay Street, Schenectady, 346-4902. This is the place for anyone who smokes, with offerings of tobacco, cigars, and pipes.

Powdertech Custom Powdercoated Finishes: 4779 Duanesburg Road, Duanesburg, 356-1322. Got any old, rusty lawn furniture? Or maybe a small airplane? They can make anything of any size look new again. And they're nice people too!

Screen-It Ltd.: 668 Hoosick Road, Troy, 272-1606, 1-800-641-1606. Whether it's your artwork or theirs, the service is always professional, fast, and friendly. If you need a cheap wardrobe and don't mind wearing someone else's logo you can get overprints for super cheap.

The Troy Book Makers: 282A River Street, Troy, 689-1083. No one willing to publish your book? Publish it yourself. They will guide you through the process and feature your book in one of their local bookstores.

The Water Garden Co. (part of Eddie's Aquarium): 898 New Loudon Road (Route 9), Latham, 783-3474. Do you want a peaceful pond in your backyard, but are just too lazy to do all the work to get it? These guys will do it for you, or can fix the one you have and make it a working mini-ecosystem.

Things You Shouldn't Do But Will

Body Modification

The Dead Presidents Lounge: 1092 Madison Avenue, Albany, 689-0730.

Lark Tattoo: 278 Lark St, Albany, 432-1905. Get a tattoo, then head over to Soho's across the street for some pizza while you regret the tattoo.

Lark Vegas Piercing Co.: 273 Lark Street, Albany, 434-4907.

Tom Spaulding Tattoo Studio: 628 Central Avenue, Albany, 482-6477. This has been a fixture on Central since 1978.

Adult Novelties

Amazing.Net Adult Video & Magazine Center: 516 River Street, Troy, 272-7577. This is the spot for adult videos and magazines with a selection of adult novelties.

Deja-Vu: 145 Wolf Road, Albany, 459-6495. This shop features smoking supplies, exotic lingerie, and adult novelties.

Romeo's Gifts, Inc.: 299 Lark Street, Albany, 434-4014. Not only a gift shop, but an erotic supplies store, too.

Route 20 News and Video: 275 Columbia Turnpike, Rensselaer, 479-3415. Offers adult videos and magazines, and a selection of adult novelties

WOOF!

Did You Know?

Lord Cornbury was a *very* unpopular governor of New York in 1707, a post he also held in New Jersey. He was universally disliked in both states and in 1707 was being arraigned for bribery and corruption in New Jersey. According to the *Albany Chronicles* written in 1906, in a letter from a Lewis Morris to the New Jersey secretary of state in the middle of 1707 he comments, "I must say something of him [Cornbury], which perhaps nobody will think it worth the while to tell. He dresses publicly in woman's clothes everyday, and puts a stop to all public business while he is pleasing himself with that peculiar but detestable maggot." Now we thought this might be some kind of 1707 joke, but no, if you Google images, the first picture to come up of Lord Cornbury, is a painting of his Lordship wearing a lovely blue gown. This portrait hangs in the New York Historical Society. Of course all of this—the letter and the painting—could have been "leaked" by unhappy colonists to discredit Cornbury before the British government.

Event Calendar

Albany, although a smaller version of a real city, still offers up some big entertainment, at a small-town price. We have some outstanding yearly events and venues that get you close up to some of your favorite performers. The following is a list of sources to guide you to some of the good stuff.

Annual Events

January

Friday Art Nights: Its cold. You could just stay inside, however, the Friday Art Nights go on all year.

Winter Festival and Ice Fishing Contest: Grafton Lakes State Park (www.friendsofgraftonlakes.org).

February

Dance Flurry in Saratoga Springs: Dance your way across the town (www.danceflurry.org).

New York in Bloom at the State Museum: A true breath of fresh air in winter (www.nysm.nysed.gov).

Schenectady County Winter Carnival: Maple Ski Ridge (www.schenectadycounty.com).

March

Northeast Great Outdoors Show: Empire State Plaza Convention Center (www.edlewi.com).

St. Patrick's Day Parade: Downtown Albany. No explanation needed; wear your green and get free ice cream at Stewart's.

April

Sit back and watch the tulips grow.

May

Colonial Re-enactment: Mabee Farm, Rotterdam Junction (www. mabeefarm.org).

Tulip Festival: Washington Park, Albany Held on Mother's Day weekend, the festival is glorious in every way.

June

Art on Lark: Lark Street in Albany This is a friendly street fair with lots of good local art and crafts. Check www.albany.org for specifics.

The Clearwater: Pete Seeger's sloop, The Clearwater, sails up the Hudson River during the summer months to remind everyone what a treasure the river is and what we need to do to take care of it. The Great Hudson River Revival Festival takes place in June in Croton Point Park down river, but the sloop makes an appearance in Albany later in the summer. Look for it. Sail on it. Enjoy the river on it (www.clearwater.org).

Father's Day Pops Concert: The concert features the Albany Symphony at the amphitheater across the Hudson River Way. This is a free concert followed by fireworks. It's a great gift for your dad and it won't cost you a dime.

Flag Day Parade in Troy: Marching along Fourth Street, this is the biggest parade anywhere. Visit www.troyny.gov for date.

The Gallupville Gas Up: Taking place on the second and third weekends of June, the Gas Up features antique engines doing all sorts of things, old-time steam shovels, old farm machinery, all running in a field in Gallupville.

Troy River Street Festival: The festival features art and music in downtown Troy.

July

Free music in Albany: Riverside Park. Alive at 5 on Thursdays. Fun, fun, fun.

Canalfest or more precisely the Lock7-12 Canalfest: History, concerts, water fun, tours, games, and fireworks—this is our Erie Canal. Get out and enjoy it! (www.lock7-12canalfest.com).

Park Playhouse: The playhouse starts its run of free musicals at the Lakehouse in Washington Park. These are professional quality productions and they are FREE!!! (www.parkplayhouse.com).

Saratoga Race Course: The racecourse opens for the season in the last week in July.

Troy's "Pig Out": This BBQ competition has only been around for a couple of years, but it is so popular we imagine it will just keep getting bigger and better. This competition rounds up some of the best BBQ teams from all over (but mostly New York state) and features music, crafts, and FABULOUS food running over 2 days.

World Team Tennis at the SEFCU Arena: 1239 Washington Avenue No. 3 on the University of Albany Campus, 1400 Washington Avenue, Albany (www.nybuzzwtt.com).

A number of craft and other festivals are held in July so check www. albany.org, *Metroland*, or the *Times Union* Preview section on Thursday for a complete listing.

August

Time to start your back to school shopping.

September

Irish2000Fest: Saratoga County Fairgrounds. This is a 2-day festival with nonstop music (www.irish2000fest.com).

Larkfest: This is Larks Street's end of summer extravaganza with food, music, crafts, and FUN (www.larkstreet.org).

Scottish Games at the Altamont Fairgrounds: The beginning of September (Labor Day weekend) brings us the Scottish Games. Men in kilts throwing logs—need we say more?

Stockade Art Show: Schenectady's Historic Stockade District. This art show usually is held Labor Day weekend, but check the newspaper for the exact date.

Uncle Sam Parade in Troy: Visit www.troyny.gov for date and location.

Waterford Tugboat Roundup: Waterford. The roundup is usually the weekend after Labor Day, but make sure to double-check. More than 2 dozen old time tug boats are open for touring and there's music, food, kids fun stuff, and fireworks (www.tugboatroundup.com).

October

Apple Festival and Craft Fair: The Altamont Fairgrounds. More than 150 crafters and APPLES!!! (www.northeastshowpro.com).

Columbus Day Parade: Downtown Albany.

Goold's Orchard's Apple Fest: Goold's hosts its annual Apple Fest on Columbus Day weekend with music, crafts, local wine, and of course delicious apples.

November

Capital Holiday Lights in the Park: Washington Park, Albany. The lights shine until January.

Capital Region Holiday Parade: State Street, Schenectady. This is the largest nighttime parade in the northeast down. Our very own Santa Claus parade.

Shaker Heritage Society Annual Craft Fair: Held in the meeting house, this craft fair takes place from the beginning of November through Christmas week for stress-free shopping.

December

Annual Holiday House Tour in Albany: The tour gives you the opportunity to peek inside a dozen of Albany's historic homes decked out for the holidays (www.historic-albany.org).

First Night: On December 31, Saratoga hosts a wonderful First Night throughout its beautiful downtown.

Santa Speedo Sprint: The sprint runs down Lark Street in Albany. Sponsored by the Albany Society for the Advancement of Philanthropy (ASAP), the sprint supports local charities (www.albanysociety.org).

Victorian Stroll in Downtown Troy: Get dressed up like your great-great grandma (or grandpa) and head down to Troy for some music and entertainment. Enjoy shopping, eating, the lights, and more.

WinterFestival: Downtown Albany. Visit www.albanyevents.org for a rundown of planned performances and activities.

Ongoing

Remember!!!!

Albany' First Friday: www.1stfridayalbany.org

At the Warehouse/Albany Flea: 20 Learned Street, behind the Miss Albany. The Warehouse and flea market continue to offer a small range of antiques, crafts, and food, as well as architectural salvage. The warehouse is open on weekends with some weekday hours (check the Web site: atthewarehouse.net) and the flea market is open outdoors every Sunday 10 a.m. to 4 p.m. (www.albanyflea.com) from June through the beginning of October. Plenty of parking is available.

Friday Art Nights: All year long; all fun, all different.

Schenectady Greenmarket: A year-round farmer's market right in downtown offering a wide and delicious selection of fresh produce, cheese, meats, milk, baked goods, etc. During the summer the market is located at City Hall, 105 Jay Street; in the winter it moves inside Proctor's on Robb Alley and the Education Center. It is open Sundays from 10 a.m. to 2 p.m. (374-1956).

Schenectady's Art Night: Schenectady's Art Night is held the third Friday of each month (www.artnightschenectady.org).

Troy Night Out: This event is held the last Friday of each month (www.troynightout.org).

Troy Waterfront Farmer's Market: Bringing you fresh produce, milk, cheese, meats, and so much more, the market is located inside the Uncle Sam Atrium on Broadway at Third and Fourth streets in Troy every Saturday through April from 9 a.m. to 1 p.m. It moves outside to Troy's Riverfront Park on Front Street in the spring, Saturday 9 a.m. to 1 p.m. (312-5749).

Current Event Sources

timesunion.com
www.albany.org
www.larkstreet.org
www.metroland.net: You can browse through their guides for food, music, bars etc., online.
www.troyny.gov

Check under our "Music to Your Ears" heading for the Web addresses of some pretty great places to hear live music and our "Go to the Theater" heading to see some live stage performances.

Calendar of Historical/Hysterical Events

Including Albany, Troy, and Schenectady

February 8, 1690: The Schenectady Massacre occurred. Indian and French entered the stockade and burned all but two houses and killed 60 men, women, and children.

July 26, 1700: Gov. Richard Coote, certain that Canadian Jesuits were training natives in the art of witchcraft to use against the allied natives, in the case of the wife of a local Onondaga, decided it "was not fit she should live any longer in the world to do more mischief; and so made it up to her, and with a club beat out her brains." Nice guy.

May 1715: In order to halt construction of St. Peter's Church on city property, an express messenger is sent *by canoe* to speak to the governor, with no effect.

January 15, 1716: Philip Livingston is born at the corner of State and Pearl. A sign marks the spot. He's important because he signed the Declaration of Independence.

April 11, 1743: Johannes Myndertse is paid a whopping 7 shillings to repair the public stocks so that Albanians could continue to look at the local criminals on their daily walkabouts.

April 28, 1752: The new city seal with a beaver on it is adopted and the old one with an ALB on it is "declared null and void and dead in law." It is interesting to note here, that once the new city seal was adopted, they starting charging everyone to place the seal on all legal documents. Of course, it was a very cute seal, with a strolling beaver with Albany written over its head. We would have paid 6 shillings just to have that stamped on any of our legal stuff, too.

September 17, 1755: Philip Schuyler and Catherine Van Rensselaer are married.

June 1758: The song "Yankee Doodle" was written by Dr. Richard Shackburg (a.k.a. Shuckburg, Shuckburgh) a British surgeon while American and British forces were hanging around together at Fort Crailo waiting to move north for a battle at Fort Ticonderoga. The American troops had none of the British spit and polish so Shackburg wrote the song to poke fun at the Yankee doodles (fools). Only in this case, the "fools" ended up using it as their marching anthem in their fight for independence 20 years later. Who's laughing now.

July 6, 1758: Lord Viscount Howe is killed at Fort Ticonderoga during the French and Indian War. Philip Schuyler, who considered Howe to be one of his greatest friends, brings his body back to the Flatts in Watervliet and arranges for his burial, which is located under St. Peter's. He has moved with the church and is still buried in the entryway. He was greatly admired by both the British and American troops. He was 34 years old.

March 1763: Albany's second fire truck arrives from England, costing the city $397.50

1767: According to the *Albany Chronicles* of 1906, this was the year Albany decided it was time to stop buying English goods due to their extremely high duties. The beginning of the end.

December 14, 1780: Alexander Hamilton marries Philip Schuyler's daughter Elizabeth.

March 4, 1781: George Washington is named godfather of Philip Schuyler's daughter Catherine at her baptism.

August 7, 1781: The Schuyler tomahawk in the balustrade story begins. Out to kidnap Gen. Schuyler, a band of Tories, Canadians, and Indians break into the Schuyler Mansion. As the Schuyler clan ran for safety upstairs, daughter Margarita ran back downstairs to save her baby sister Catherine. Running back upstairs she barely misses getting hit with a tomahawk that ends up stuck in the balustrade. They do not manage to get Schuyler but did make off with some of the family silver. The Schuylers never got it back, but it was reported that their soup tureen was seen on a dinner table in Montreal a few years later.

January 4, 1792: Albany citizens start collecting funds to erect a college, which would become Union College.

February 3, 1792: The upper crust of Albany meet at Robert Lewis' City Tavern to discuss starting up a bank.

February 10, 1792: The above-mentioned group decides to name the bank the "Albany Bank."

February 17, 1792: The proposed bank starts selling subscriptions at $15 per share at the City Tavern.

February 27, 1792: The Albany Bank elects its board of directors, which basically includes all of the upper crust citizens who proposed the idea of a bank 3 weeks earlier. Abraham Ten Broeck is elected president on June 12, 1792.

April 10, 1792: The "Bank of Albany" is incorporated.

May 14, 1793: The Bank of Albany pays out its first dividends—$4.25 per share

November 17, 1793: One of the largest fires in Albany's history wipes out 26 houses along Broadway and Maiden Lane (including Ten Broeck's earlier mansion). The fire starts in Leonard Gansevoort's barn. Three slaves were charged with starting the fire and are hanged.

February 1794: Bank of Albany shares are now going for $400 each.

July 12, 1794: Flames consume James Caldwell's chocolate mill—lucky flames.

December 14, 1794: Erastus Corning is born.

February 25, 1795: Union College is founded.

April 30, 1795: The temperature is recorded at 14° below zero. Brrrrr.

October 1796: Whipping posts are abolished in the city of Albany.

October 1796: The Arch St. Brewery is established on Arch Street in Albany. This would later become the Albany Brewing Co.

September 5, 1807: Robert Fulton's steamship, the Clermont, is the first steamship to dock in Albany.

December 28, 1831: The "Marble Pillar" building at the corner of State and Broadway opens for the Thorpe and Sprague stagecoach lines. It also housed a museum collection and was called the Museum Building for years. It became the Albany Trust Company's building in 1904 (with a reworking by architect Marcus Reynolds).

September 11, 1847: John Boyd Thatcher is born. He served as mayor of Albany from 1886 to 1888.

August 17, 1848: "The Great Fire" of Albany, started by a washerwoman's bonnet (you cannot make this stuff up) destroys 600 buildings, 37 acres of land, and causes $3 million worth of damage. Jealous fire companies riot 2 days later leading to the death of a fireman from a gunshot wound.

July 9, 1851: Jenny Lind (the greatest living singer of her time) performs at the Third Presbyterian Church in Albany.

October 1, 1851: The first train of the Hudson River railroad arrives from New York City.

June 10, 1854: A law to prevent pigs from running loose on Albany's streets is finally enforced after 50 years or more on the books, resulting in the capture of 15,000 pigs, much to everyone's surprise.

July 21, 1854: Temperature measures 100° in the shade.

November 7, 1855: All of the "Know Nothing" candidates win at election. The Know Nothings was a political party fearful of the large number of Catholic immigrants (mostly Irish). They believed the immigrants would be more loyal to the pope rather than to the U.S. government, but we suspect that it was a bit more than that. In 1854, the Know Nothing party became the American Party. By 1860, the American Party was no longer and most of its members became Republicans.

September 13, 1863: John Taylor, owner of the largest brewery in the United States dies. He served as mayor of Albany from 1848 to 1849.

December 1886: The Empire Curling Club is organized.

January 15, 1888: The Ice Palace is built at the corner of Madison and Lake avenues. There is a picture of this in the children's orientation film at the Albany Visitor's Center. It is very cool (pun intended!).

September 29, 1893: The Moses statue is dedicated in Washington Park. This was a gift to the city from Henry I. King in memory of his father Rufus H. King.

January 1, 1899: Theodore Roosevelt is inaugurated as governor of New York.

April 8, 1901: The John Van Schaick Lansing Pruyn Free Library is dedicated. This historic library, designed by Marcus T. Reynolds, was built on the site of Pruyn's birth in a modified Dutch Renaissance style with imported Holland Dutch fireplace tiles from 1540 and other fabulous pieces from Europe. It was actually demolished in 1968 to make an entrance ramp for I 787 during the construction of the Empire State Plaza. Way to go!

July 1902: Dr. Milbank brought the first automobile to the city for professional purposes.

Did You Know?

Cuyler Reynolds, who wrote the *Albany Chronicles* 1906, where we obtained most of our dates and odd facts, was the older brother of Marcus T. Reynolds, who designed the fabulous D&H Railroad Building/SUNY Plaza building (as well as the demolished Pruyn Library). Cuyler was the first curator of the Albany Institute of History and Art, and also one of Albany's great historians.

The Smalbanac's Guide to the Solar System

Looking at the night sky is free—at least so far—and you can actually see it from Albany. Take some time to enjoy it. Without a telescope you can see Mercury, Venus, Mars, Jupiter, and Saturn at different times of the year and you can enjoy meteor showers almost every month. Here is a quick guide to our eight planets, and some of the smaller ones we share the Solar System with.

The Sun

The Sun is the star in the center of the Solar System. It is not the biggest or the hottest star in the universe, but it seems to work perfectly for us. The Sun is a giant ball of gas (72% hydrogen, 26% helium, and 2%

heavier stuff like nitrogen, oxygen, and carbon). We get heat and light from the Sun due to nuclear fusion. When random nuclei of hydrogen bump into each other and merge helium is produced and a whole lot of energy is released. The Sun has been doing this for about 4.5 billion years and is expected to keep right on doing this for another 4.5 billion years. It has a diameter of 864,000 miles, dwarfing anything else in the Solar System. Although it is about 400 times the size of the moon, it is also about 400 times as far away, so to us here on Earth, the Sun and moon look to be about the same size. The Sun does not have a formal name like other stars in the sky. It was called Sol, the sun god and the Solar System is named for it.

The Planets

There are eight planets in the Solar System: Mercury, Venus, Earth, Mars, Jupiter, Saturn, Uranus, and Neptune.

Mercury

Mercury is the small planet closest to the Sun. It was named for the Roman god Mercury who was the winged messenger to the other gods (and he was very fast). Because Mercury could be seen moving around the Sun so quickly this seemed a very appropriate name. Thousands of years ago, the Greeks thought Mercury was actually two planets, one visible at dawn and the other at dusk. The morning planet was called Apollo and it wasn't until the fifth century BC that Pythagoras realized they were one and the same. About 30 years ago, the Mariner 10 Spacecraft came close to Mercury and gave us more information. Mercury is called an inferior planet because it is between Earth and the Sun. This also makes it hard for us to get a good look at it because it is usually lost in the glare of the Sun. It is only visible for up to 2 hours before dawn or after dusk and only at certain times of the year. These times are when Mercury is at its greatest elongation—or when it appears to be furthest from the Sun from Earth's vantage point. Mercury is about 36 million miles from the Sun and only takes 88 days to go around it.

Venus

Venus is the second-closest planet to the Sun. It is named for the Roman goddess of love and beauty because of its brightness in the morning and evening skies. Like Mercury, Venus also was thought to be two planets, the morning star Eosphorus and the evening star Hesperus. (Astronomers knew it was just one planet early on). Also, like Mercury, Venus is an inferior planet located between Earth and the Sun. The first spacecraft to visit this lovely planet was Mariner 2 in 1962. Because it has a thick cloud cover, information was gathered using infrared technology. It was once thought that Venus was Earth's twin, looking to be about the same size and makeup. However similar the planets might have been early in development, Venus is nothing like Earth and is probably the most inhospitable of all of the planets. The closeness to the Sun boiled away any liquid there might have been and greenhouse gases sealed its fate. Venus' atmosphere holds in the heat of the Sun making it hotter than Mercury. It is about 67 million miles from the Sun, and its "year" is 224.7 Earth days. Inferior planets never appear fully lit and appear to us in phases like the moon. Venus, being one of the brightest objects in the sky, has often been mistaken for a UFO because of this. A very bright, oddly shaped light in the sky must be a spaceship.

Earth

Earth! We live here which is an amazing fact all by itself. Earth is located about 93 million miles from the Sun which makes us neither too cold nor too hot. Somewhere in our distant past it is suggested that an asteroid hit the Earth, which gave us our water source. Seventy percent of the Earth's surface is covered in ocean and 80% of all photosynthesis takes place in these oceans. Earth is the only planet in the Solar System that is not named after a Greek or Roman god but rather is named after what it is—earth or ground—from the Old English *oerthe*. Originally it was believed that Earth was the center of the Solar System, an idea pushed by Ptolemy in the second century. It wasn't until 1543 when Copernicus, a Polish astronomer, came up with the model placing the Sun in the center of the Solar System. Originally thought to be flat, it became apparent looking at the Earth's shadow crossing the moon during eclipses that it indeed was a round planet. The Earth has a wonderful 23-degree tilt that allows us to have seasons as we orbit around the Sun. At the center of the Earth is a core of nickel and iron. This, combined with its motion, creates a dynamo producing the magnetic field. The Earth's diameter is 7,926 miles and its year lasts 365¼ days. We also have one beautiful moon.

Mars

Mars is the fourth planet from the Sun and the last of the terrestrial or rocky planets before we hit the asteroid belt. Like all of the other planets (except Earth), Mars gets its name from a Greek or Roman god. Ancient cultures associated the red color of this planet with blood and so named it after the Roman god of war, Mars. (The Greeks named their god of war, Ares). Although only about half the diameter of Earth, Mars is most like Earth. It has almost the same tilt, giving it very similar seasons; its day is only 30 minutes longer than ours. It is about 50 million miles further from the Sun than the Earth so every season is much colder and longer (its year is 687 days long). Mars has two smallish moons (most likely captured asteroids, rather than left-over planet material) named

Phobos and Deimos (fear and panic—the Greek names for the dogs—or children of Ares). Mars also is home to the highest known mountain in the Solar System—Olympus Mons—as well as the largest canyon. Mars has frozen polar icecaps that are easily seen with a telescope. Sadly, no Martians have been found by either the Rovers, Spirit, or Opportunity, or by any of the orbiting satellites.

Jupiter

The first planet on the other side of the asteroid belt is the largest planet in the Solar System. Jupiter is named for the Roman king of the gods (the Greeks called theirs Zeus). In the night sky, Jupiter is brighter than most stars and is easily seen without a telescope. It is so big that it would take 1,000 Earths smooshed together to equal it. Unlike the four closest planets to the sun, which are rocky, solid spheres, Jupiter is an enormous ball of gas and liquid. Even though it is so large, it spins faster on its axis than any other planet, having a day that lasts only 9 hours and 56 minutes. The surface is marked with beautiful ribbons of different-colored clouds (all caused by different chemicals at different heights). The Great Red Spot of Jupiter is one of its most outstanding features. It is a reddish-brown, swirling storm that has been viewed for more than 300 years. The spot itself has a diameter three times larger than Earth's. On its trip to Pluto, the New Horizons spacecraft found a smaller red spot, which was nicknamed Little Red. Jupiter has 62 moons, some having eruptions that shoot hundreds of miles into space. Jupiter also has three wispy little rings near its equator. Jupiter is 483 million miles from the Sun and takes 11.86 Earth-years to orbit it.

Saturn

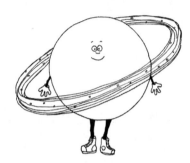

Saturn is the second largest planet in Solar System and the sixth from the Sun. It also happens to be most people's favorite because of its beautiful rings. Saturn has thousands of rings, which were first observed by Galileo in 1610. Every 15 years, the Earth passes through the plane of Saturn and faces the rings edge on. Which means, the rings seem to vanish. This happened in 2009 so the rings are still pretty thin but will gradually get broader as we go through 2010. Saturn's name is from the Roman god Saturnus—the same god as the Greek's Kronos or Cronus, the Titan god who ruled time and the ages. Kronus also is the god who ate all of his children, except Zeus. Saturn's long and majestic trip around the sun (almost 30 years) was the inspiration for its name. Although its chemical makeup is much like that of Jupiter, its distance from the sun, at 886.7 million miles, makes it cooler and the chemical reactions have less pizzazz. Saturn has more than 60 moons, 52 of which have formal names.

Uranus (UR uh nus)

William Herschel discovered this planet in 1781 and named it the "Georgian Sidus" after King George III of England. The name Uranus came into use in 1850 when it was thought that we should keep the theme going and name it for one of the Greek or Roman deities. Uranus was the name of the Greek's earliest supreme god, son of Gaia and father of Cronus. Uranus is the seventh planet from the Sun and the third largest by diameter. It is considered an ice giant, composed mostly of rock and ice. Whereas Jupiter and Saturn are mostly hydrogen and helium, Uranus is only about 15% hydrogen. Looking through a telescope, you can see its beautiful blue-green color and its sideways rotation. Uranus has a diameter of 31,814 miles, about four times that of the Earth. Uranus has 11 known rings and 21 named moons (and a handful of no-names). Most of its moons have Shakespearian names, which in a lot of cases are named after mythological characters, kind of like the planets. Uranus is 1.783 billion miles from the sun and takes 84.01 Earth-years to orbit it.

Neptune

Once Uranus was found it became apparent that there must be another planet out there, messing around with Uranus' orbit. So, the hunt was on for another planet. On September 23, 1846, Neptune was first observed by Galle and d'Arrest at the Berlin observatory using French astronomer Le Verrier's calculations. Using calculations from English astronomer Adams, Challis at the Cambridge Observatory, observed Neptune almost at the same time. Adams and Le Verrier were given equal credit. The name Neptune, for the Roman god of the sea, was suggested by Le Verrier and recently, papers suggest that it was Le Verrier's work that really found the location of Neptune and that Adams was quite a bit off. In any case, Galileo really saw it first, in 1612. Neptune is the eighth and last real planet in the Solar System. It again is an ice giant, having a higher content of water, ammonia, and methane than either of the gas giants. It owes its deep blue color to trace levels of methane. Its diameter is 30,198 miles, just slightly smaller than Uranus. Neptune has faint rings like Uranus and 13 known moons. It is 2.793 billion miles from the Sun, and takes 164.79 Earth-years to orbit it.

Pluto, Dwarf Planets, and Plutoids

We like Pluto, so we are going to talk about it as though it is still a real planet. Pluto was discovered by chance by a 23-year-old Kansas astronomer named Clyde Tombaugh who had just arrived at work at the Lowell Observatory in Arizona in 1930. He found it by comparing photographs to see if any objects seemed to change position in a 2-week period. Pluto did. Venetia Burney, an 11-year-old Oxford girl who was interested in mythology, named it Pluto, which is another name for Hades, the god of the underworld. The name became official on March 24, 1930.

Pluto is a very tiny planet. It has a 1,429-mile diameter or 18% of the Earth's. It also takes a very elliptical path around the Sun, a trip that takes 247.69 Earth-years and passes inside Neptune's orbit for around 20 of those years. This last happened between 1979 and 1999. Before that, about 150 years ago. Pluto has one very big moon named Charon, which it fights with for dominance in its orbit. It also has a couple of little tiny moons that we have only just recently found. The spaceship New Horizons is on its way to Pluto and in 2015 we should discover a lot more about this planet.

When we started to discover more planet-like objects out there, the International Astronomical Union decided it was time to recategorize things and Pluto's place in the Solar System changed (figuratively). With the discovery of the small planet Eris in the Kuiper belt and wondering what to do about Ceres, the larger-than-Pluto asteroid, it was decided to make a new grouping called *dwarf planets*. So, in 2006, poor Pluto got demoted. Then in 2008, the IAU decided to create another grouping called *plutoids*, basically any planet-like object past Neptune. So now, Pluto is not only a dwarf planet, but also a plutoid and a plutino—a whole other story. At this writing we have one, "just a" dwarf planet, Ceres, and a number of dwarf planet, plutoids, which include Pluto, Eris, and Make Make. (Make Make was discovered during Easter time in 2005 so the name was taken from Easter Island meaning "the creator of humanity").

Fun Things You Can Look for in the Sky!!

Meteor Showers!!!

Meteor showers occur when the Earth passes through a debris field left by a comet. They are named for the constellation that they seem to fall from, not for the comet they came from. We can see them following pretty regularly. And always on or within a day of these dates.

January 3–4 Quadrantids: There used to be a constellation named the Quadran Muralis in the northeastern sky, which is what these were named for. The constellation was eliminated from the lineup, but its stars are still there near Bootes and Ursa Major (the great bear—look for the big dipper).

April 21–22 Lyrids: Near Lyra the harp.

May 4–6 Eta Aquarids: Near Aquarius.

July 28–29 Delta Aquarids: Also near Aquarius.

August 12 Perseids: Near Perseus.

October 21 Orionids: Near Orion. Are we catching on yet?

November 16 Leonids: Near Leo.

December 13 Geminids: Near the Gemini twins.

Web Sites for You to Visit

www.skymaps.com: This will give you the monthly goings on of the stars and planets.

http://stardate.org/nightsky/: This is from the University of Texas' McDonald Observatory and is a great Web site containing tons of information.

http://www.seasky.org/: This is a Web site put up by an excellent amateur astronomer and sea lover named J.D. Knight. Again, lots of fun information here.

www.nasa.gov/: You could spend days here seeing what's up with the universe.

Science 101

A nautical mile was based on the circumference of the Earth. If you take that measurement (24,901.55 miles) and divide it by 360 degrees and then 60 minutes you get a distance of around 1.152 miles or 1,852 meters. Basically, you could measure a nautical mile by taking a minute of the arc of any great circle around the Earth, but as we are not a perfect sphere this measurement was not exactly the same everywhere. The measurement of 1,852 meters per nautical mile is the universal standard today.

Some of Our Sources That We Are Willing to Reveal

Albany Visitor's Center

Astronomy magazine

Encyclopedia Britannica: the real one that sits on a bookshelf

First Church

Historic Albany Foundation

http://nightsky.jpl.nasa.gov

The Hudson Through the Years by Arthur G. Adams

In and Around the Capital Region by Ann Morrow and Anne Older

Mayor Erastus Corning: Albany Icon, Albany Enigma by Paul Grondahl

The Mentor: The Story of the Hudson by Albert Bushnell Hart (August 1, 1917)

Metroland best of guides

Philip Hooker by Edward W. Root

See Albany magazine

St. Mary's Church

St. Peter's Church

Ten Broeck Mansion

timesunion.com

Troy Visitor's Center

Waterford Harbor Visitor Center

Wikipedia

William Kennedy's "O Albany"

www.1stfridayalbany.org

www.albanybarn.org

www.answers.com

www.danceflurry.org

www.famousamericans.net

www.nysm.nysed.gov

www.pbs.org

www.rkstar.com

www.smithsonianmagazine.com

www.space.com

www.thomasgraz.net/glass

www.troyfoodcoop.com

www.volunteermatch.org

See, we didn't make it all up!

Index

198   Index

The Smalbanac can be reached at **smalbanac@gmail.com** or **www.smalbanac.com**

Some people weren't quite sure who *this* was supposed to be. Since we use him all over the Smalbanac, we thought we'd let you know it's not Shakespeare. It's supposed to be Henry Hudson, hence the monogrammed HH on his shirt or cape. Hope this clears up the confusion.